Mary Ellen Sterner Wagner

HEALING HIDDEN MEMORIES

Mary Jane Williams

Health Communications, Inc.
Deerfield Beach, Florida

Library of Congress Cataloging-in-Publication Data

Williams, Mary Jane
   Healing hidden memories: recovery for adult survivors of childhood
abuse/by Mary Jane Williams.
     p. cm.
   ISBN 1-55874-107-0
   1. Adult child abuse victims — Mental health. 2. Women — Mental
health. 3. Adult child abuse victims — Rehabilitation. I. Title.
RC569.5.C55W54   1990
616.85′ 822 — dc20   90-4651
                                                                          CIP

©1991 Mary Jane Williams
ISBN 1-55874-107-0

All rights reserved. Printed in the United States of America. No part of this
publication may be reproduced, stored in a retrieval system or transmitted
in any form or by any means, electronic, mechanical, photocopying, recording or otherwise without the written permission of the publisher.

Publisher: Health Communications, Inc.
              3201 S.W. 15th Street
              Deerfield Beach, Florida 33442

Cover design by Graphic Expressions

Dedication

Within every person who has survived childhood sexual abuse is a wounded child: a child afraid of people, a child cowering in the corner, a child who takes the blame of the rape, a child who is not cared for, and a child who hates herself and sees herself as ugly. Until our wounded child is healed, the person holding that child within us will never be whole. This book is lovingly dedicated to all the people who are courageously healing their inner wounded child.

Acknowledgments

I would like to give my heartfelt thanks to the following people who have been my guides from time to time on my journey of healing.

To Suzanne, my loving daughter who has filled our time together with love and light.

To Ben Ohrenstein, my dear, loving friend, who knows the meaning of friendship and lives it every day. Also a special thanks for untiringly helping me edit this book.

To Melinda Miller, my dear friend and colleague, who has taught me about energy and who has lovingly shared her knowledge with me.

To Mariah Fenton Gladis, therapist par excellence, who taught me to acknowledge and love my inner wounded child. Also thank you for introducing me to Gestalt therapy and dreamwork.

To Twylah Nitsch, who so lovingly taught me the Seneca Indian way of living and allowed me to join her on her earthwalk. I honor you for talking your truth.

To June and J. D., for the love that they were able to share. And to Alice who provided balance.

To Jacob Schwartz, who keeps my eyes on the stars.

To Chad Breeze, who, although he neither talks nor walks, has taught me about love and has altered my course in life.

To Nancy Nicholson, who shares her life so generously.

To Marie Stilkind and Jeff Laign, for being able to see my vision before it was fully formed, and for their kindness.

Contents

Introduction

Healing Hidden Memories is a book about my own journey from the darkness of the pain caused by childhood sexual abuse into the light of recovery. My journey has changed over the years since I began to heal.

From a solid grounding of several years of Gestalt therapy I branched out into different types of healing. I found that the sexual abuse damaged more than just my psychological mind; my spirit and my body were also affected. I learned that more than psychotherapy was needed to help heal my whole being.

As I wrote this book I discovered that the chapters fell into three categories: "The Journey Home," "The Journey into Light" and "The Journey of the Heart."

The largest section of the book, The Journey Home, concerns the multiple wounds of childhood sexual abuse. I look in detail at each wound. Additionally, three threads weave their way through most of the chapters in this section: healing the inner wounded child, healing through dreams and healing with the energies of the earth.

We were all wounded as children and we continue to carry the wounded child within us. Until our inner child is healed we will remain disconnected to our present life and our lives will be fragmented. The second thread found in the chapters is dreams. Dream analysis is useful to heal the inner wounded child because the dream forms a bridge between the past and the present. The third thread that is woven into the tapestry of the book is healing with energy — the energies of color, sound and visualization.

I believe the human body, mind and spirit are made of energy. Scientists have discovered that energy cannot be destroyed. However, it can be changed. The energy of fear can be changed into the empowering energy of love. The pain of abandonment can be transformed into a solid, secure sense of self. Life-long patterns of self-hatred can be changed into self-worth.

Part Two, Journey into Light, gives a more detailed account concerning the healing energies of sound and light. Dreams, courage and forgiveness are seen from the point of view of recovery.

Part Three, The Journey of the Heart, looks at the wounds of society and how the imbalance of male and female energies on this planet earth have contributed to sexual abuse of children.

In order for the reader to understand part three I would like to explain how I use the words male/masculine energy and female/feminine energy. When I speak in the book of men and women, I am referring to the actual human being. When I speak of male or masculine energy or female or feminine energy, I am not referring to the human being but, rather, I am referring to the energy on this earth that has feminine characteristics or masculine characteristics. Both men and women have masculine and feminine energy, masculine and feminine characteristics.

Feminine energy has certain characteristics or properties. For instance, think of the womb, the uterus. The uterus has a cycle of waxing and waning like the moon. Each month the uterus builds up tissue in preparation for the nurturing of a fetus. When the egg is not fertilized, the uterus releases the nourishing material to prepare for another cycle. The main tasks of the uterus are to receive, to nourish and to release. These are characteristics of feminine energy.

On the other hand, masculine energy is very different. Think of the sperm which has activating, penetrating energy. These are masculine characteristics. In order for life to continue on this earth a balance is required between activating/penetrating energy and receiving/nurturing energy. Both energies are necessary. Both energies are important and both women and men can cultivate these energies within themselves.

Also, I use the words *darkness* and *light* as archetypal images. These words represent ancient symbols that originally came out of primitive cultures observing the changes through which the earth moves. Darkness represents night and winter. Likewise light represents day and summer. If there were no night, the earth would scorch. If there were no winter, there would be no time of rest.

Winter is a time of going within. Night is a time when the world is not easily seen. The survivor has a place within herself that is not easily seen. Her journey into light teaches her to go within and shine the light of day on her inner darkness. Just as there needs to be a balance between male and female energies so, also, there must be a balance between darkness and light.

Throughout the book I used the feminine pronouns, *her or she,* to refer to the survivor. I was trying to avoid the awkwardness of saying *she or he,* as well as attempting to reverse the age old *"he"* seen in most books. Also, there are several places in the book where I refer only to women simply because that is my experience. The men reading the book will need to reverse the gender in those examples.

There is an old Sufi tale of nine blind men touching an elephant. Each man is sure that he is the one who "knows" what an elephant looks like. One man is touching the tail and one man is touching the foot and another man is touching the softer underbelly. Each man is accurate about the part of the elephant he is touching, but none of the men knows what the entire elephant looks like.

This is how I feel about this book. I am one of the blind men touching the elephant of recovery. Through my own journey I have happened across ways to heal the survivor of childhood sexual abuse but they are simply some of many. I have included a variety of approaches in the book in order to appeal to people at various stages of growth. If you do not feel that you understand what I mean by *color healing,* then simply read on until something feels familiar. You are your own guide and if some of the things I have discovered on my journey are helpful to you, I am pleased. Take what feels good and put the rest aside for the moment.

PART ONE

The Journey Home:
The Wounds

1

The Inner Wounded Child

Dream

I was taking care of a beautiful, well-kept house. The owners had a mentally retarded, psychotic young boy. It was my responsibility to take care of the boy but I did not know that when I took the job. The family came back once and left a sitter with me to help care for the boy. The next day the sitter took me to see the child's school. It was like a zoo, with bars and cement slabs.

When we came to the cage of the boy we were caring for, he turned into a small child and became a girl. The little girl voluntarily crawled into the cage; she crawled down a cement incline and curled up on the cement slab. I was looking at her through locked bars. I began to cry deeply and was very sad. The sitter asked why I was crying and I answered, "No wonder the child is psychotic. It's so incongruous, to live in such a nice house and to come to a place like this for school."

All survivors of childhood sexual abuse carry within themselves an inner wounded child. Acknowledging and healing the inner wounded child is the foundation, the underpinnings, from which all other healing springs. In the beginning of the healing process it feels impossible to look at the wounded child within us. The journey to heal our inner wounded child is difficult because we have separated ourselves emotionally from the pain of the abuse. It takes great courage to look within and to face our inner wounds.

Some of the wounds of the inner child are guilt, abandonment, terror, non-communication, a feeling of being different, a feeling of ugliness and a sense of dying. Is it any wonder that frequently it is so difficult to look at that child?

When we have been deeply hurt, we long for other people to take care of us and to love us. However, in truth, no one else can heal our inner wounded child. We have to do it for ourselves.

Our wounded child is a part of ourselves that we do not like, that we criticize and reject. Until we realize what our wounded child looks like, we do not understand why we dislike ourselves. This inner core of pain is a direct result of the abuse.

> *"I don't like you," I said to my inner wounded child. "I thought I would never have to see you again. I thought I had put you so far away that I would never have to deal with you and your pain again. You're the one who did something wrong so many years ago."*

I did the above dialoguing with my inner wounded child in the beginning of my Gestalt therapy. It was the first time I had ever acknowledged her, and I discovered that I greatly disliked her. I was repulsed by her . . . to look at her made me angry. I was surprised to realize that it felt as if there was no place in me that could reach out to her. I had previously not even been aware that I was blaming little Mary for the rape. By relegating *bad little Mary* to my subconscious mind, I had been able to function out of *good little Mary* in my everyday life. In order to survive I had totally rejected the child who had been raped and molested. She was no longer a part of me — or so I thought.

To heal, to be happy in the world and to live without the pain, this inner wounded child must be brought out into the light and loved and healed. I have used three principal methods to help heal my inner wounded child: working with dreams, dialoguing with my own inner wounded child and visualization. My dreams have revealed to me, with painful accuracy, the damage done to my inner child. The healing started when I began talking with her and then visualizing her healing.

Dreamwork

The dream at the beginning of this chapter is one of my many dreams concerning my wounded child. In this dream the wounded child was mentally retarded and psychotic. I had been taking care of someone's house but had not bargained for taking care of their wounded child. The house in the dream was beautiful and well-kept and was symbolic of the outer me, the me that on the surface was successful and competent. However, in the dream I then discovered how this wounded child really lives. The wounded child changed from a boy to a girl who looked like I did when I was five and was raped. The little girl lived like an animal in a cage with bars and cement slabs and was not mature enough to walk.

In the dream, as I recognized my internal wounds, I found myself becoming very sad. As I saw the incongruity of how the child was treated, I realized what I had done to my own inner child.

> *"I'm sorry. I didn't know what I was doing. I left you there all alone and didn't realize that would be hurtful. It wasn't your fault. You didn't cause it to happen. All these years I've blamed you and have kept you hidden. I'm so sorry."*

Actually saying this to your inner wounded child is essential in order for healing to occur. We have all blamed our inner child for rape or other abuse. We have all blamed ourselves at the time the abuse occurred. It is now time to learn to forgive ourselves.

The following dream occurred after I had been in therapy for a brief time:

> I was taking care of a small disabled child. I left her with someone else and I believed she would be safe with these people. When I returned she was hanging on a hook on a wall, almost completely wrapped in a cocoon. I was astonished that these people had not taken care of her and had almost allowed her to die. I took her off the hook and unraveled the strands of the cocoon. I apologized to her. She looked up at me with obvious thankfulness.

The child in the dream looked like me when I was five. In the dream, however, the child was disabled: She could not walk or talk. I had left a child who could neither run away nor tell anyone if she was mistreated with people who were not trustworthy. This is exactly what happened to me at five when I was raped and molested: my parents had left me, just for a few hours, with a man who could not be trusted.

The cocoon in which this child was wrapped was like the cocoon a spider wraps around a fly, trapping it until the spider wants to eat it. This cocoon was about dying, not about transformation.

In both of my dreams my inner child was severely disabled. As I worked with these dreams I began to realize that the disabilities had two meanings in my real life. First, of course, the level of disabilities reflected the extent of my own wounds but, secondly, I began to get in touch with the fact that children who are severely disabled need a great deal of care and love to grow and to change. In both dreams I had not taken proper care of the children and I was not taking proper care of my own wounded child.

Gestalt therapy teaches that the dreamer is represented by each and every part of the dream. I was the cocoon which was killing my inner wounded child. I was the dying child. I was also the family who abandoned the child and the cold cement slab that gave no comfort. I was the uncaring hook that did not allow for change. I was the sadness and the realization that something was wrong. I was the person who rescued the child in the cocoon and I was the thankful child. As I began to dialogue with the different aspects of myself, I began to heal.

Until our inner wounded child is healed, she lives with the fear of the abuse which is always potentially life threatening. If our wounded child is afraid, then we are also afraid. Living with constant fear, without trust and without being able to communicate, is what happens to the survivors of childhood sexual abuse. We were touched so brutally that some of us never want to be touched again.

Beginning The Dialogue

Our inner wounded child will not come to us, we have to go to her, over and over again. Our wounded child lives in the past and, until we dialogue with that child, she is never connected with the present. The wounded child is always the age when the damage occurred and she never matures until we rescue and love and help that child to grow.

When we learn to dialogue with our inner child we find our inner wisdom. Often our child will tell us what is needed if we will only listen. Listening is important for the survivor to do because our wounded child needs to communicate with us. It may be the first time in many years that our inner child has had an opportunity to talk. We were warned not to tell anyone and, therefore, we all have a great deal of trouble with communication. If we allow our wounded child to heal and to begin to talk to us, then we will, in turn, be able to talk more effectively in our world.

It is not a simple task to heal the wounds of childhood sexual abuse. Many times you will find that you have worked and worked and then hit an unbearably painful wound. It may take more energy than ever before to rescue your wounded child again but each time you bring your wounded child back to heal the wounds, you will find you are becoming more whole.

The skills needed to heal your wounded child are truly fairly simple. Imagine yourself meeting an abandoned little child who is afraid and lonely. What you would ordinarily do for this helpless stranger is just what your own inner child needs. You may pick her up and say comforting things to her. You may want to buy her something to eat or new clothes to wear. You may want to assure her it was never her fault that she was wounded in the first place. The reality of our lives is that it is frequently easier to help a stranger than it is to help ourselves.

Begin to please your inner child as if she were a living and breathing person because that is just what she is. Take her for walks, sing to her. Buy your child toys and dolls. Comfort your child when she is scared. Laugh with your child when she is happy.

The truth is that we did not create the act of our having been raped or molested. The truth is that a very sick person did this because of his or her own darkness. And the last truth is the most difficult to accept: We are the ones, the only ones, who can now pick up the pieces for ourselves and heal the inner wounded child. Other people can be there as guides, as friends, as therapists but the work has to be done by us, the survivors. We are the ones who have to get up every morning and deal with our pain and we are the ones who have to turn to our child in pain, holding and loving that child the way she should have been held and loved years ago.

Healing Tools

I have found music to be healing. For instance, *Lullaby*, sung by Chris Williamson, has been a wonderful song to play over and over again as I have visualized holding my wounded child. I was first introduced to this song at Gestalt workshops I attended for several years. I have found it helpful to make a tape of the song and play it several times in a row so that I can sit in a rocking chair and rock my inner child as I play this beautiful lullaby for her. Also, I have found that using ear phones has enhanced the experience; it has created a very special healing space. As I visualize holding my inner child, I see us bathed in a beautiful indigo blue light. Indigo blue calms and takes away negativity.

Rocking stimulates the parasympathetic nervous system, which in turn soothes the body and assures it that everything is all right. As survivors of sexual abuse we are all too familiar with the opposite part of our nervous system, the sympathetic, which stimulates fear, flight and fright. We need to stimulate the soothing part of our nervous system and we need to inhibit the fear/flight/fright which has become a part of our lives since the abuse.

Another song I have also used is Joe Cocker's *You Are So Beautiful*. Instead of imagining someone else, however, I have visualized my inner child standing in a beautiful green light.

Green is the color of the heart chakra and is a very healing color. As you begin your visualization make it as detailed as possible. See your inner child as how that child looked before having been abused. Sing the song to your child, over and over again. Your inner child should be surrounded by the green light as well as by your healing words. You can alternate the colors of yellow, light blue, indigo blue and violet for different forms of healing.

Ask your inner child what color she wants. Learn to trust your child. She knows what she needs. As you learn to trust yourself and your inner voice, it will guide you through your journey of healing.

If you are having trouble connecting to yourself as a child, dig out the old photographs and find pictures of yourself before, during and after the abuse. You may have to call relatives or friends but the effort will be worth it. Just the act of finding the pictures will be healing. Take the pictures with you to therapy and begin to remember who you were.

When I found my old pictures, I was astonished. Before I was raped at five by a visiting minister, I was well cared for and had matching dresses with my mother. After the rape my hair was chopped off like a waif and I wore hand-me-downs. On some unconscious level my parents agreed with me that I was damaged goods. No one knew I had been raped but they treated me differently after that.

Use the image in the picture to dialogue with and learn to send love to that child. Frame the picture and put it on your dresser. You are worth it.

Moving Toward Wholeness

After you have found your wounded child and the healing process has started, you will begin to find an inner peace and strength. The more time you are able to spend with your inner child, the more quickly you will become whole.

The lives of survivors can be very complicated with intricate weavings of abuse continuing in their lives. The key to change is to take one strand, one thread at a time. One of the threads is the inner wounded child. As you take that one thread you will begin to unravel the web of abuse. Courageously acknowledge your inner wounded child, heal her with dialogues and visualizations, and the threads of abuse will be broken.

2

Abandonment

Dream

I was being forced to leave my home. I was not allowed to take anything except a few clothes. I had to leave my parents and all my belongings behind. Outside, there was devastation everywhere. It looked like the landscape after a nuclear holocaust. I wandered through the ruins, feeling lost and alone.

Healing abandonment can be a very confusing part of the healing process because, in truth, we were abandoned by our father, by our mother and, for a great many of us, by the rest of the family as well. For the most part, however, the pain of abandonment seems to be concentrated around the abandonment by our mothers, making it hard for us to see the entire cycle of abandonment.

A paradox about a woman who has been sexually abused as a child is that she is openly angry with her mother while at the same time the anger toward her father is hidden. Generally the mother is blamed, not the father. In part, this is because the child has experienced violence at the hands of the father and to be angry at him is not safe.

Another piece of the puzzle is the phenomenon that happens when a child is abused and the abuser is still a power figure in that child's life. The child assumes the guilt of the act, thereby making it safe for the child to continue to live with this person who could abuse her again. The child takes on the sins of the father.

I believe it is even a little more complicated, however. Feminine energy is nurturing energy; it is renewing and caring. I believe much of the anger directed at our mothers occurs because our mothers were not capable of caring for us and we desperately needed, then missed, that care while growing. We realized that feminine energy was missing in our lives and we were angry about it. In my case, as I am certain in many others, I could see other children receiving the feminine love and care that my mother was not capable of providing and it hurt me very deeply.

The Incestuous Family

My mother was fairly typical of the mother in a family of incest. There is usually a deep lack of self-worth in the woman who allows incest in her family. The lack of self-worth is so deep that the woman often feels too inadequate to impose discipline. She feels she does not have the right to tell someone else what to do. Very often she feels so inadequate that she is uncomfortable with the role of mother and gives up the duties of being a mother to the children, thereby setting the stage for incest. The mother often knows the father is raping the children but her self-image is so poor she can not risk trying to confront or to stop it. She believes she is emotionally and economically tied to her husband and she feels she has no choices. She aligns herself with her husband instead of with her children.

Usually the relationship between the mother and the father is verbally abusive. Their relationship is frequently built on the superiority of the man. The woman who already has no self-worth puts up with constant reminders she is not worthwhile. The image of the man being superior is not based on his self-worth either. In fact, it is also based on a deep lack of self-worth. Sometimes the only thing that makes the man feel good about himself is to feel superior to his wife. His self-image is derived from outside of himself, not from an inner sense of self-worth.

When there is a deep lack of self-worth in the woman, her experiences of making love and her sexual experiences in general are often not fulfilling. She either relinquishes that role in the marriage or never sets limits on the frequency of the sexual activity. Neither of these choices necessarily lead to incestuous families. For incest to occur, the rest of the puzzle lies with the father. The father who sexually abuses his children has done damage to his system of boundaries, in combination with other problems.

Telling Mother

While trying to understand my anger at my mother and my feeling of abandonment, I remembered a time a few years ago when I decided to face my mother with my hidden past. The conversation was going like most phone calls with Mother — badly. Conversations between us had never been easy. I had not told Mother yet about my hidden childhood.

On this particular day, Mother seemed more upset than usual about us not getting along. I had not seen her in over three years, largely because I did not know how to tell her about my childhood sexual abuse. I was not certain if she would believe me and I did not know how I would react if she accused me of lying. I had not reached a place of resolution yet concerning my mother. I was still holding on to my anger toward her.

The first five years of my therapy had not been effective because I had become involved with a nonprofessional group of people. By the time I later began Gestalt therapy, I had been working very hard but without the proper tools. The only progress I had accomplished during those years was to uncover the memories. By looking at my painful childhood without the benefit of good professional help, I had actually made some of my problems even more difficult. One of the wounds that had not healed was my anger at my mother. I was holding on to my anger at my mother at all costs. At the time I did not know what the final cost would be.

Finally Mother insisted we talk about what was wrong between us. I gave in and said, "Mom, I know why our relationship has been so difficult but I don't think we should talk about it on the phone." I was living in Pennsylvania at the time and Mother was in California.

For some reason Mother was insistent that day and kept saying she wanted to know. At last, at long last, I decided to tell her.

"Mom, do you remember when you went to California that last year we lived in Oklahoma?"

"Yes," Mom quietly answered.

"While you were gone," I continued, "Daddy came into my room while I was asleep and raped me." A long silence followed.

"You were different when I came back and I asked you what was wrong but you said nothing was wrong," Mom said with a strained voice.

"Daddy had threatened me. He said he would kill me if I told you." Mom began to cry.

I did not give her any more details because I could tell she would not be able to hear and it seemed cruel. Mom started talking, trying to remember that time in her life. Mom always had the ability to say very important things in a simple way, showing she had no understanding of their impact.

"Your father told me once he wanted to have sex with you but I didn't believe him" she said absent-mindedly.

I turned cold. I could not believe my own ears. Knowing my father had a mental disability, my mother had left me with him, even though he had said he wanted to have sex with his own daughter. I could have stayed with a friend or my sister or even a member of the church because my father was a Methodist minister at the time. She had choices.

"There's more, Mom," I added quietly on the phone. "Do you remember me asking about the visiting minister a few years ago? He also raped and molested me. I don't know where you were but he molested me in a bedroom in the house where we lived when I was five."

This was too much for Mom to handle. She believed me but it was a reminder that she was not a good mother if her daughter had been raped two times. She was never able to remember this part of our conversation after that.

About five months later I purchased tickets to visit Mom in California but 14 days before I was to leave, my mother died. I never saw her after that phone call. I had held on to my anger at all costs and the final cost left me with more anger.

My mother died before I could resolve things with her. Letting go of my anger toward my mother felt as if I was saying being raped was not wrong. As long as I held on to my anger, I held on to what little dignity I had left. If I had abandoned my anger prematurely, I would have abandoned my wounded child within and would have fallen into despair. The timing of my healing and the timing of my mother's death were not the same. I have since resolved my relationship with her.

The Oedipal Dilemma

There are many pieces that make up the puzzle of abandonment. Some of the pieces are fear of the father, carrying the guilt of the father, loss of feminine love and support, loss of the love of the father and abandonment of our own inner wounded child.

The definition of "abandon" in *The Random House College Dictionary* is "to leave or forsake completely and finally." When our fathers or stepfathers raped us, they did forsake us, completely and finally.

I was not in contact with the abandonment by my father until after he died. I had been acutely aware of Mother abandoning me but I had not realized that at 15 I also lost my father. I never got him back. I had lost the love of my father as if he had died. Even though during the last few years before he raped me, he did cruel things to me, he still had not completely abandoned me, he had not completely sacrificed me.

This loss of love from the father is very complex. The normal father-daughter relationship is forever injured and this injury follows the woman as she tries to build relationships. When the father has crossed the line and become sexual with his daughter, the child is placed in a very real dilemma.

During my therapy I remembered having a fantasy a year or two before the rape occurred. My father and I were dancing and we danced into forever, happily ever after. In my fantasy my mother did not exist, my happiness was with my father. Then a year or so later, I was raped by my father. My fantasy came true! I never wanted it to come true; the fantasy was merely an innocuous flight of the mind of a young adolescent and, while not overtly sexual, the fantasy has hidden seeds of sexuality. This Oedipal dilemma set the stage for a great deal of pain and abandonment for the woman survivor.

I got my father! What should have been simply a fantasy of a normal growing teen had become a nightmare. It is not difficult to understand that I carried enormous guilt for the actual enactment of my fantasy in real life. A teenager should fall in love with her father but if the father crosses the boundary line, the daughter cannot help being stuck at the age of the enactment of that fantasy. Instead of growing from loving the father to being in love with the boy next door, the woman who was raped by her father experiences shame, guilt and rejection by the father and sometimes will continue to have hidden sexual relationships that end in shame and rejection.

When the father no longer abuses the child sexually, he abandons her, he discards her. It is this abandonment that becomes a central theme for that woman survivor, a familiar pain that continues to be re-enacted but, for the most part, remains hidden to the survivor. The girl child realized her wish, her fantasy came true. She, in essence, married her father and "killed" her mother. This is the ancient story of Oedipus from Greek Mythology, except when it is the child who is raped by her father, it is the father who acts out the fantasy not the child.

I believe this Oedipal dilemma sets up the child for abandoment from both parents. The father abandons the child twice; the rape is the first abandonment and he abandons her again when he stops using her sexually. The mother is caught between two issues. She has already passively abandoned the child but now the child, out of guilt, cuts off the mother. Psychologically the child cannot handle what has happened. Even though the child was not re-sponsible in any way, she is stuck with the guilt. Every time she looks at the mother, she feels guilty because she slept with her mother's husband.

One way this frequently is played out by the adult survivor is to fall in love with married men or women or have affairs while still married or in some way have a hidden love affair. A key to understanding the Oedipal dilemma is that hidden sex, unattainable love and rejection become a repeatable pattern in the life of the survivor. It becomes a hunger from that moment on, only instead of being hungry for a relationship that will be fulfilling, we become hungry for a relationship that carries unattainable love, hidden sex and rejection. It is at the moment of rejection that we are then satisfied and go back to the same lover or to a similar type lover, for the cycle to start all over again. We camouflage the hunger that was originally created by the rape and try to get it from unavailable men or women. Emotionally unavailable people are also attracted to us by our hunger.

We cannot change our father, we cannot change the incident and we cannot change these unavailable people with whom we think we are in love.

What we can change is our reaction, our response to the trauma.

No matter how many times we try, we will not be able to get love from emotionally unavailable people and the amount of pain we feel when they abandon us is directly proportional to how much we have healed this Oedipal dilemma.

Healing this hunger needs to be accomplished with a trained and skilled therapist. The guilt around this issue can be very potent and dangerous if handled badly. Self-forgiveness will result from our healing of our guilt. Truly we have done nothing wrong. We richly deserve our own forgiveness. As you learn to release the guilt and shame, you will find that you are making different life choices. You will no longer pick sexual partners who give you shame and rejection.

I believe that the confusion concerning abandonment is derived from the fact that the survivor rarely sees the whole picture. It is a very painful picture to view. We were abandoned by everyone: Our father raped us, our mother permitted it to happen in some fashion and other members of the family saw us from that moment on as damaged goods.

Abandoning The Inner Child

To add to the confusion, we promptly abandoned our own inner wounded child. An enormous feeling of isolation and loneliness became our constant companion. From then on we drew people to us who continued to abandon us. The cycle would be repeated over and over. This can be a dangerous cycle because, with many of us, wanting to die is part of it. After the rape we wanted to die, and each time we are abandoned, the memory of wanting to die returns and we find that we are facing our darkness again. (I have dealt with the problem of suicide in the chapters "Thoughts of Suicide" and "Tools to Release Thoughts of Suicide.")

The key to healing the pain of abandonment first requires us to go within ourselves and heal our own inner wounded child. Before anger can be effectively expressed, before fear and guilt can be released, we must stop the abandonment at the very center of ourselves. We must no longer abandon our own child, that child we have blamed for so many years. This is probably the hardest thing a survivor must accomplish because we do not know how to love that inner child. We know how to reject her, we know how to hate her and we certainly know how to ignore her but we do not know how to love her. Part of our inability to love our inner child can be traced back to our mother who, because she did not know how to love herself, was never able to show us how to love.

Hidden Strengths

Years ago a Gestalt therapist told me about a study done with monkeys. Immediately after birth the experimenters took the female babies from their mothers. The babies were raised without mothering of any kind. They were given food and water but were not loved in any way. When the babies reached the age for mating, they were introduced to male monkeys. Many of the female monkeys did not know how to mate. The females who did actually mate had babies and it was this generation of monkeys that were followed in the study.

These deprived mothers were found to be incapable of mothering their children. They were not affectionate; they totally ignored their babies. The babies of the deprived monkeys divided into two groups emotionally. One group had autistic type behavior and just wandered around aimlessly, unable to learn their normal skills. The other group was known as "the pokers." They would poke their mother until she gave them some response. The response might be negative, such as hitting the baby in return, but the baby wanted some attention from the mother and apparently anything would do.

These "pokers" continued to poke their mothers until they had shaped the behavior of their mothers. The babies who had enough spunk to poke their mothers received mothering in return, albeit not the best in the world, but at least they did receive something. The "pokers" grew up to be better mothers than their own mothers. The other group never appeared to change.

I was definitely a "poker." At three I ran away from home because I wanted to go to church without my shoes on. Later, when my family was quite dysfunctional, I would methodically, day by day, do little things to my mother until she would get angry with me. It sometimes took me days to get a response but as soon as I made her angry, I would turn away and smile. Until I learned of the study of the monkeys, I never understood why I smiled. I poked my mother until I got a response, and then I was happy.

When my family no longer gave me affection, I would obtain it from other families. For several years I would spend more nights at the homes of friends than at my own. I would take love wherever I could find it.

I suspect that if you have expended the time to read this book, you are also a "poker," and that somewhere along the line you have already learned something about nurturing. I recommend that you take your nurturing skills and now concentrate them on your inner wounded child.

If you have reclaimed and loved your inner child, you will be able to reach that hidden anger at the perpetrator, the man who raped you and took your childhood from you. There is probably no rage to compare to the rage that you will unleash when you face the perpetrator with your healed child at your side, for it was never your fault and you know it now for the first time in your life. When you are in therapy and are united with your inner child, put your father in front of you and put the rage where it belongs.

After your rage at your father is released, you will find less anger toward your mother because some of it was misplaced anger. You are now free to get to the real anger at your mother. Beneath that anger is a great deal of sadness for the love you never received. I found that when I was finally free to see clearly my anger at both my parents, there was a qualitative difference in the type of anger I carried for each of them. There was deep rage at my father, which had been covered over by terror. With my mother the anger was softer and laden with sadness.

As survivors of childhood sexual abuse, we find the abandonment by our mothers has cut us off from feminine energy, from the source of who we are. As we reclaim our wounded child and our own inner womb, we are healing that abandonment, we are recovering our femininity.

As you learn to love your inner child, you will find you have broken the cycle of abandonment. You broke it yourself by loving yourself!

3

Hidden Memories

Dream
When I Was 15

I was lying in my bed in the house we lived in at that time. My father was standing over me and attacking me, and I was fighting him off. It was not until I was 35 that I discovered it was not a dream, that I had uncovered the real nightmare I had been so afraid to remember and had relegated to my subconscious mind for 20 years.

All memories of childhood sexual abuse have to be hidden because the act has to be hidden. This cloaking, this concealment, is the glue that holds the web of abuse together. As the hidden memories are revealed, the glue dissolves and healing becomes possible.

Every child who is abused sexually is told not to tell. Every child is threatened to keep the memories hidden. The threats that the perpetrator uses are different for each child but whether you were told you would be killed or that pictures of the act would be shown to your family and friends, the effect is the same: The child does not tell.

This not telling, this secret we all have held, makes us an accomplice to the act — an unwilling accomplice but, nevertheless, an accomplice. The perpetrator knows it. It is how he keeps the child in submission.

Being an accomplice makes it difficult to admit to the abuse. It also makes it difficult to retrieve hidden memories. Often only one or two children in a family where all of the children were abused are able to talk about it and admit to the abuse. I believe one of the major factors that keeps these children from telling the truth about having been abused is the enormous guilt arising from being an unwilling accomplice to such a horrible act.

Keeping the memories hidden keeps the guilt intact and the web of abuse from unraveling. Keeping the abuse hidden contributes greatly to the continuing cycle of abuse. Many perpetrators were themselves abused as children but because their guilt was so overwhelming, they were never able to look at the memories and heal their own inner wounded child.

Cloaking The Memories

There are many ways to keep the memories hidden. My memories were completely occluded until I was 35, which helped to make the abuse play a very strange part in my life. On one hand I had no memory of the abuse but, on the other hand, pieces of the abuse were part of my everyday life.

Fear of the dark, fear of opening my mouth for the dentist, disgust with the smell of beer on someone's breath are but a few of the pieces of the abuse that I remembered. By keeping the memories hidden, I lived a disconnected life. I did things and said things and felt things with no understanding behind the doing or the saying or the feeling.

If I were awakened in the middle of the night by my lover to make love, I would respond with anger and hate: I found out much later that my father wakened me in the middle of the night to rape me. When the dentist would work in my mouth, I was gripped with fear and had difficulty breathing: I remembered under hypnosis that the visiting minister molested me by ejaculating in my mouth when I was five. If someone kissed me with beer on his breath, I was filled with disgust: My father had been drinking beer when he raped me. Until I remembered the rape at age 35, I would lie in bed paralyzed with fear whenever I was alone in the house.

These were all memories of the abuse but until I could remember and admit that the abuse actually happened, the memories not only were disconnected from my past but also made me disconnected with my present. Because the act had to be hidden, anything which occurred in my present day that reminded me of the abuse immediately became disconnected and fearful.

People who were abused over a long period of time cloak the memories of the abuse differently than I did. The memories, for the most part, are available to their conscious mind. However, their memories are believed by them to be unimportant to their present life. These people have so strongly disconnected themselves from the abuse that the memories are, in a sense, also hidden, even though they are remembered.

People who have hidden their memories in this manner are often in therapy for a long period of time before they realize the abuse affected them and they are able to tell the therapist about it.

Recalling The Memories

An example of how the mind recalls these painful memories happened to me several years after I had first remembered the abuse and had begun working on healing the memories. A thought kept coming to my mind: "They are going to find out I'm not a physical therapist." The fear that came with this thought was enormous and almost paralyzing. Even though the thought was not founded in reality, the fear was so overwhelming that I was upset for days. In actuality, I was remembering what it was like when I was 15 and was deathly afraid that people would find out that I had been raped. This is one way the mind discloses a hidden memory. Only a piece of the abuse is revealed and as the thought becomes conscious, it attaches to something in the survivor's present life, sometimes totally unrelated.

Another very current example is that when I began writing this chapter, I became quite upset and extremely resistant to writing it. I was very depressed and the thought kept repeating in my mind that there is no one I can tell. This came to me over and over until the light finally dawned: I was remembering another piece of the aftermath of the abuse. When I was raped there was no one I could tell and, as I was confronted with looking at the hidden memories again, more hidden memories surfaced. I often feel as if there is no one to turn to when I am sad or depressed. That, however, is simply a memory and not a reality in my life today.

One of the difficulties with retrieving hidden memories is that the pain of the abuse always accompanies the memory. As the thought comes to the conscious mind, the feeling is also retrieved. Many people resist remembering because of the emotions that are stirred up by the memories.

It has been my experience, however, that we feel the pain whether or not we remember the incident. By repressing the abuse, we experience pain in our lives by being so disconnected with both our past and with our present.

Denial

If the survivor is disconnected with the pain of the abuse, then frequently she also is disconnected with pain in her everyday life. This can create a situation whereby the survivor unwittingly puts herself in a position where she can be mentally or physically hurt.

Several years before I remembered the hidden memories, I was responsible for placing myself in a position where I could easily have been raped again. Luckily it did not happen. I was never able to understand why my judgment was so poor until I began to heal my childhood wounds. Simply said, my judgment was poor because I was not in contact with the deep pain that I had experienced. I was not in contact with myself. If I can deny my past pain, then I can also deny any possibility of pain in the present.

To keep the memories hidden, I had to deny a large part of myself. I had to deny that I was raped. I had to deny that I lived in a severely dysfunctional family. I had to deny the hatred I felt toward my parents. I had to deny that I hurt.

This degree of denial created a considerable amount of conflict inside myself. Living with this much denial caused me to begin to doubt who I was. I could no longer trust myself because I had become part of the lie. I could not tell the truth about my parents.

It was more important to me to believe in my parents than to tell the truth, even if it meant making myself wrong and untrustworthy. This allowed me to continue to live in a fantasy world where I believed I had wonderful parents and a happy life.

One of the costs of living in this fantasy world was that it necessitated I become and stay very controlling. The more that had to be hidden, the more I had to control. I had to carefully manipulate my world to keep the truth from becoming known. After a period of time, I no longer remembered the abuse but I still needed to control. The fear of being found out was a strong motivator. The real issue was to control my own mind, to control my memories. But to control my memories I also had to control my outside world. "If I control you, then you will never find out the secret I am holding."

Hypnosis

At one point in my therapy I agreed to undertake hypnosis to bring back the memories of the rape when I was five. One of the insights I gained concerned the visiting minister who had threatened me not to tell my mother. Through hypnosis I found out that at five I was so confused by the rape that I had decided not to tell her anything for fear of telling her the wrong thing. As I grew up and forgot the rape, I was puzzled about why I could not tell my mother anything. But I never relented.

This is an important issue that occurs in families where the rape was inflicted by someone outside of the family. After the rape or molestation or abuse, the child completely changes the way she communicates with the family. The child's ability to talk and to share even the smallest personal things has been dramatically impaired. It is like the monkeys who hear no evil, see no evil and speak no evil. Rather than speak evil thoughts, no thoughts are spoken at all.

This inability to speak severely damages the relationship between the child and her family. It is bad enough that the rape itself was extremely damaging to the child, but now a different level of pain also occurs. Because of the secrets held by the child, a wall becomes erected that few parents have the skill to work through without professional help. Having to hold the secrets isolates the child and deepens the pain.

Using Care With Hypnosis

At this point let me hasten to share with you a cautionary note on the use of hypnosis in retrieving otherwise unavailable memories. When I used hypnosis to bring back the rape incident which occurred when I was five, I remembered not only the incident itself but the terror and the desire to die as well. The memory of the desire to die became such a part of me that for a week or two after the hypnosis I could not separate myself from the thoughts of suicide or my inability to tell anyone in order to ask for help. If you and your therapist decide that the use of hypnosis might be helpful, it must be very carefully monitored with extra therapy sessions and a slow approach to your regaining of the memories.

Beginning Therapy

Beginning therapy for a survivor of sexual abuse can be a very frightening and confusing time because the memories are still hidden. For years the survivor may have thought of her past as though it did not matter. In your therapy, pieces of the past will begin to be revealed and confusion will result. Your confusion is very healthy but it can be very frightening. Your confusion will be a direct result of your beginning to make connections from the present to the past. What was previously not available will begin to surface. The glue holding the memories together as a secret will be dissolving. The awful secret will be in the process of being told.

Wanting to quit therapy can be a temptation. You felt better before you started therapy, relationships seemed to work better before therapy. "It must be the fault of the therapy!" Allowing the hidden memories to surface is not pleasant, but our healing occurs by finally facing our pain.

When the survivor begins therapy, she is "taking power" in her life, probably for the first time. This act could unbalance her relationships. It may seem to her and/or to her partner that the therapy is only causing trouble. If both people in the relationship can see that it is simply a change and that equilibrium can be found again, then less fear will get in the way.

As the survivor begins to look at the hidden memories, fear, anger, shame and many other emotions will surface. The survivor needs to be supported at this time more than at any other time.

In some instances, the partner of the survivor may demand that therapy be ended because the partner will be too frightened of the changes brought on by therapy. This demand will put the survivor in a difficult situation. At this point she has only begun to look at her past and a part of her also probably wants to quit. However, if she quits therapy to save the relationship, she will be abandoning her inner wounded child again. This abandonment will only leave her in more pain. Also we all have the model in our memories of our mothers staying with the perpetrator instead of taking care of us. This lack of good modeling in our lives makes it difficult to resist lifelong patterns.

There is also a readiness for therapy that needs to be respected. If you truly feel you are not ready for therapy yet, then respecting your own feelings may be a step forward for you. Look deep within your heart and follow what it says.

Discovering Memories

When you are ready to work on hidden memories, there are many techniques that can be used to help in remembering the abuse.

One that may work is to simply write freely without making an effort to think. First, write single words in a column. Write them as quickly as possible with as little conscious thought as possible.

Fill pages upon pages and then look at them with your therapist. Discuss the words, the pauses and the relationships of the words.

Your abuse will creep into the column of words and you will then be able to take more of the abuse into the light of day.

Another avenue into the past is through your dreams. Your dreams will show you the disconnectedness of your life. You will have the opportunity to integrate your past and your present. (Please refer to the chapter "Windows to the Self" for more on dream analysis.)

Begin to keep a journal. Jot down in it your thoughts and feelings that occur to you during the day, even though they may not seem to make sense to you. It is all part of the puzzle of the abuse and it is important to connect it in your mind. I remember visiting a home of a friend and saying to myself that their daughter should not dress in such a sexy way in front of her father. Another memory trace that I have had is the feeling of big wads of cotton in my mouth as a child. This is a direct memory of being molested at five. I still cannot have cotton in my mouth at the dentist's office.

Having my own child has inadvertently brought up hidden memories for me. At the time I gave birth to my daughter I was not in touch with my childhood abuse. However, I was very uneasy about having a child and felt greatly relieved that I gave birth to a girl. I knew somewhere deep inside myself that I could not be as loving toward a boy but I did not know why. Also, as my daughter has grown into puberty and has become very attractive, I have had to face more of the pain of my own abuse and fear of my own sexuality.

When the occasion arises and it becomes necessary to leave your children with a caretaker, unexpected fear can arise. This fear can be a real clue if you happen to still be wondering whether you were abused or not. If you have a strong fear of leaving your child, it could very well be that something happened when your mother left you. A good place for you to start your inquiry is to explore what you believe might happen to your child if you leave her or him.

Sexual activity is another area where hidden memories surface. What should be a loving, enjoyable experience of sharing love with another person is often a painful experience of having hidden memories surface. Loving touch can be misinterpreted by the survivor of childhood sexual abuse.

Some of the difficulties I have encountered have been excessive cystitis after intercourse, passivity, disinterest, pain with touch, pain with intercourse, feeling of suffocating, fear, lack of feeling in my vagina and many times just wishing it were over. For the most part, however, I am pleased to say, most of these problems are not part of my lovemaking anymore. I have had shiatsu massage even in my vagina to help release the painful memories. I have also lovingly touched myself, visualized healing in that area and become very careful about who I have as my love partner.

The Cost Of Hiding

When a person has hidden memories, a great deal of energy is used in keeping the memories hidden. The day after I remembered the abuse for the first time, I felt as if I had been drugged. So much of my energy had been used to hold the memories of the abuse in place that when the memories were finally released, the energy was also released. It felt as if my muscles were being pulled into the earth. My movements were slow and I was very sad and confused. I wanted to talk about it to people but I felt more disconnected than ever. I felt as if I were between two worlds — the past and the present — but I did not feel like I belonged to either world.

This uncomfortable period can be part of the picture of recovery but with support and guidance you will regain your equilibrium again. Warm baths, soothing music, kind friends and talking about the abuse with safe people you trust will help you through this hard time. Being good to ourselves is difficult because most of us do not know how to do it. (Please refer to the chapter on "Tools to Release Thoughts of Suicide" for more ideas on taking care of yourself.)

A generalized loss of memory also can be caused by hidden memories. When your mind is busy not remembering the abuse, sometimes other items are forgotten also. Forgetting test items, appointments or names can be a part of hiding the past. Many times the survivor feels dumb or stupid because her memory fails her from time to time. This has plagued me in my relationships. Whenever tension has developed in a relationship, I found later that I would not be able to remember anything my lover said. I would become afraid of the possible anger (which felt like the abuse) that my mind would frequently go blank. My partner would later tell me that he felt I did not care about him when I could not remember what was said.

Incomplete Memories

Some survivors try to retrieve hidden memories and are frustrated because they are only able to remember bits and pieces of the abuse. Your subconscious mind will not release the material if the conscious mind is blocking it. One woman I know constantly has said, "I can't remember. It's just not coming back." She still is unaware that she has been telling her unconscious mind she does not want to remember.

If you are in therapy and you are ready to uncover more of the hidden memories, I suggest that you begin a dialogue with your unconscious mind and tell it that you are ready to remember. Make certain you are not continuing to make the negative statements of not remembering. Then record every dream, as well as every word or phrase related to your childhood that comes to mind.

At one point in my therapy I began to wonder what I was like when I was a teenager and what it was really like to live in my household. That night I had a dream that was probably an actual memory of how my father treated me (aside from the rape). With the dream I was then able to remember my hatred and confusion in my family of origin.

Our memories are available when we are ready to experience them.

We can control how quickly the memories return. It is usually not helpful when the memories return so rapidly that it is impossible to integrate them. Again, dialogue with your unconscious mind and tell it how much you are willing to remember each day.

During this period of remembering, proper rest and nourishment are essential. Many survivors are workaholics. If the memories start bombarding your conscious mind when you are overworked and tired, there will be no time for integration of the past with the present. That can lead to an unnecessary amount of fear in the survivor's life. The releasing technique — the "Let Go" — is described in the chapter on boundaries and I believe you will find it helpful for releasing memories and any emotion associated with them. It is not necessary to process every memory in therapy. Many of them can simply be released.

The reward of retrieving hidden memories is that our mind then begins to heal. Instead of remaining disconnected and confused, we will find that we have allowed ourselves to experience and release the memories and the pain. Through this release we hope to connect ourselves to ourselves and become whole again.

4

Anger

Dream

Two groups of people were at war with each other — a long-standing war. I was on one side of the river and was very afraid. I had a gun but someone stole it. I became angry that it was stolen and demanded another one. I was given a large rifle.

In the beginning of the dream, the river was blue. Each bank was sandy and a little barren. People were lined up on each side of the river, shooting at each other. I shot across the river but no one died.

The scene then changed. Green trees were now in the way. Several of us moved to the right in order to see the enemy better. Something strange happened, however. Many people from the other side boldly came forward to talk. I kept thinking I should shoot them, that it must be a trick. I also thought, what if it is real? One shot would ruin the peace. I had difficulty putting down the gun. Even after I had put it down, I wanted to go back and pick it up.

Both sides then walked away from the battleground to talk. I looked around feeling very alone. A woman reached out to me and we walked with our arms around each other. We were walking toward a special place in the forest, a place where there is always peace. I laughed and cried about the war being over.

Anger is a familiar emotion to every person but it is particularly familiar to people who have been sexually abused as children. Looking back over my healing, it now seems to me that the anger associated with sexual abuse can be separated into stages.

The Stages

The first stage is a generalized anger stage: There is not anything in particular but everything in general makes the survivor angry. This stage occurs before any therapy has been begun. Frequently the person is not even aware she is angry. In this stage nothing can make her happy. She is impossible to please, particularly if the opposite sex is trying to please her but, more important, she does not even try to please herself. In her mind it is not her responsibility to please herself. The survivor has so abandoned the wounded child within her that she feels she no longer has the responsibility to give herself pleasure. This is where the generalized anger comes from. At least part of the anger at this stage comes from not taking responsibility for her wounded child. If the responsibility for pleasure is projected outward onto other people, then the survivor will be constantly frustrated and angry. Passivity goes hand in hand with this ineffective anger stage; little power is taken in the world.

Stage two occurs when the survivor enters therapy and realizes she has abandoned the wounded child within her. Then the fireworks really start! It is now that the deep anger at the perpetrator usually surfaces. This is the time when hitting pillows and having angry dialogues with the perpetrator during therapy are effective. Instead of the ineffective generalized anger of the first stage, the survivor begins to return to the original experience and starts speaking out and taking power.

In this stage, considerable internal changes take place, although not too many changes are obvious yet in the survivor's life. The survivor at this stage is quietly beginning to take care of the wounded child within and probably is now having very noisy sessions with her therapist while experiencing the anger. She realizes for the first time that she can speak up when wronged and people will listen.

The second stage is then slowly overtaken by the third stage. The survivor has begun to integrate the child within herself, and she is finding that she is able to give herself pleasure for the first time in her life. Tangible changes are now beginning to be visible in her life. Some of these changes are fueled by the effective anger learned in the second stage. There is a tremendous amount of energy behind anger, and if the survivor learns to consciously use that energy in her life without harming those around her, that tremendous energy can turn into action.

Incest survivors go from passivity (a kind of lethargic, giving-up stage) to this effective anger stage. Survivors in this stage can learn to use the energy behind the anger and to take necessary action in their lives. Eventually healing will take place. The survivor will no longer be passive and will no longer be angry. She will gradually find she is taking better care of herself with greater ease. This will occur after she experiences considerable going back and forth from passivity to anger.

The Layers

Anger is a teacher but, like all teachers, it needs to be listened to. Anger is not always saying the same thing. Sometimes it is masking another feeling that is more difficult to recognize. I find the feeling underlying anger is usually fear, which I will look at in a later chapter. Also, sometimes anger is trying to tell the survivor that she is avoiding responsibility.

Recently I encountered another layer of anger. It caught me by surprise because I had stopped hitting pillows several years ago. I had been wanting to write this book but had kept putting it off with the excuse that I could not write a book, take care of my daughter and work full time. Finally, after enduring three months of a great deal of anger, I gave up and bought a word processor. The first day I began to write, my anger left. Anger is my teacher. I have had it all of my life but now instead of it ruling me and making me ineffective in my life, I understand it and use its energy. Those three months before I bought my word processor were full of channeling the energy behind the anger into taking action in the world. I accomplished a great deal of work during that time.

Transition

Sometimes anger arises during the process of therapy as an indication that the survivor is in a stage of transition: transition from an old way of being in the world to a new way of being in the world. Transition can be one of the most difficult times of growth for the survivor of incest.

A great deal of discomfort always accompanies the transition and with that discomfort comes anger: anger that you have to change, anger that you are in this position in the first place, anger that everyone else you know does not have to deal with this issue and anger that you do not have support. During these transition times— after which great changes occur in the life of the survivor—the old pain and the old way of viewing oneself continue to return. It feels at times as though you are climbing up a mountain of sand: two steps up and one step back.

Over the past years of healing myself, transition periods have been my most difficult times. Prior to the transition stage I made gains that appeared to be lost later. It is hard to keep a good perspective when it feels as if you are right back where you started. The periods of transition can and do last for months and that is a long time to feel the old pain again.

During the times of transition it is helpful to remember what gains you actually have made. Sometimes a special friend or your journal can help remind you it only feels like your old self but that you are actually changing. This is where pampering that wounded child within you can help nurture you through the difficult times. Also, if it is possible in your life, decrease your workload. Even a little less work every day can make a huge difference in how you feel about yourself. Do not expect perfection from yourself during this more fragile time. Give yourself permission to be less perfect and you will find less anger in your day.

Solidified Anger: Hate

I believe anger is healthy, particularly when it is understood and used effectively in a survivor's life. However, there is another side to anger that is very destructive—hate. Hate becomes a way of life for the child who is being sexually abused. The child learns to live on it and even feed on it. There are times that hate keeps the abused child alive.

Hatred is solidified anger and hardens the person harboring it. This form of anger, this hatred, eventually hurts the child and later adult. Even though it appears to the survivor that she is hating the perpetrator, she is really hating her own inner child. She has turned against herself.

Hatred also forms a formidable boundary around the survivor. But somewhere under that hardened boundary of hate is softness, vulnerability and enormous pain. Survivors hesitate to let go of the boundary of hate because it means looking at their own pain. It also means, somewhere down the road, looking at and owning their own femininity. The hatred hides the femininity, the softness.

Like all other patterns that a survivor learns in order to survive the continued humiliation of abuse, hatred, at one point in the survivor's life, is helpful. Once we are no longer living with the abuse, though, the hatred becomes obsolete. Letting go of the hatred at this point is not easy. It still feels as though we need it. Expression of anger, loving of the inner wounded child and being able to look at the inner pain, all contribute to the release of hate. Additionally, though, using the color lamp (see color lamp, chapter 9) and saying affirmations can have a strong impact on hate. Using the color pink in the lamp helps soften the hardened boundaries, while at the same time helps you to love yourself. While comfortably lying in the color pink, visualize yourself sitting in a river of mother-of-pearl. Melinda Miller, co-author of *Rainbow Dancer,* teaches that mother-of-pearl helps to release the past and to create transformation. Using the affirmation "I love and approve of myself" from the Louise Hay tapes also creates transformation of the pain.

Another affirmation I use from the Louise Hay tapes is "I am willing to release the cause of this" (hate). The hate is only there because we are in pain. If we are willing to release the pain, then the hate will be automatically released. If you are reading this book, the childhood abuse is over. The hate is no longer helping you to survive. It is only hiding your pain and keeping a thick boundary around you. Release the pain, build new healthy boundaries and begin a new life filled with joy and love.

5

Fear

Dream

I was with a little girl. I had taken her on a trip with me to someone's house. She was sitting on the couch saying, "But I thought you were bringing your mother!"

"No, I brought my father," I answered.

Fear came over her face and she sat farther back in the couch. She asked again, "But I thought you were bringing your mother."

"No, this time I brought my father," I answered in the same way.

At this point she became very afraid, scooted all the way back into the corner of the couch and said one last time, only now with sadness mixed with the fear, "But I thought you were bringing your mother."

I still answered the same. I didn't know what else to say to her. "No, I brought my father."

The person sexually abused as a child is very angry, but underneath the enormous anger there is another emotion. I have found
that this emotion is usually fear. I believe it is easier to deal with
anger than it is with fear and, as a result, the anger usually shows
up more often. Fear paralyzes you but if you hide your fear with
anger, at least you are able to function in the world, albeit, not with
any degree of ease.

The person who has survived childhood sexual abuse is very often
quite tough on the outside, while housing an extremely frightened
little child on the inside. The relationship of the tough outer person
and the fearful inner child is the relationship of anger to fear. Anger is
presented to the world while fear keeps the inner child paralyzed. If
the survivor has not acknowledged the wounded child within, her
tough outer image will continue to camouflage her fear.

A New Level Of Fear

The dream at the introduction to this chapter occurred ten years
after I started working on healing myself. I was visiting my father.
The dream happened on the first night in his house. The wounded
child within me, whom I had been healing for several years and had
acknowledged and taken care of, was still full of fear at the prospect
of being in the same house with my father. However, there was a
different level of fear in this dream.

The adult female in the dream, the part of me that was forging
ahead into the unknown, was trying once again to heal the wounded
child, to once again take the journey toward wholeness. The adult
female in the dream brought the father, the source of the fear, to the

little girl. The strong female inside myself wanted the wounded child to face her fear and stop hiding that fear with a camouflage of anger. The woman constantly had to repeat to the little girl that it was time to face her fear. It was time to stop living in fear of what happened 25 years ago and perhaps to develop a new relationship with the father, both within and without.

The dream was not my first indication that I was encountering another layer of fear. It has been my experience that healing occurs in layers: Looking at and healing a layer of anger allows a layer of fear to surface . . . and on and on.

I wanted to see my father again . . . I was not sure why. On the surface I wanted to visit California again and bask in its beautiful sunlight after a difficult and cold winter in Philadelphia but somewhere inside of me I wanted to face my fear of him again.

My daughter and I were flying from Philadelphia. The first leg of the trip was uneventful. However, we had to change planes in Chicago and when we checked in, I discovered I was not being given window seats. I did not think much about it. Our seats were in the middle of a wide body, with people seated on each side of us. I was fine until the very minute I sat down. Suddenly, I could not breathe and I started perspiring. I was filled with fear. I grabbed our seat assignments and ran off the plane. Out of breath, I asked for an aisle seat or a window seat. I explained I sometimes have claustrophobia and I could not sit in the middle of the plane. Fortunately for me they found an aisle seat. Feeling very relieved I returned to the plane and the breathing problems did not recur.

As the plane took off, I began to wonder about the fear. Being raped can in itself create claustrophobia in people but my father had also held a pillow over my face to stop me from screaming which made being in tight places for me very frightening. Fear . . . fear is very different to deal with than anger. A person can walk around angry but it is very difficult to move when fear grips you.

Unexpected Fear

I remember another time when fear suddenly and unexpectedly gripped me. It was a little over a year ago. I had a back injury. The doctor decided I needed a special test, an MRI. I agreed because I already had been in pain for a month and a diagnosis needed to be made. I did not take anyone with me because I had not anticipated a problem. After undressing in an adjacent room, I walked into an

oversized room. It contained a large, white, molded piece of equipment that looked like it came from a space lab. I lay down on the
cot-like table as the technician explained the procedure to me. She
then fastened a wide canvas strap over my chest and pushed a
button that moved me into a small opening in the machine. My
entire body was in the machine. Suddenly, I could not breathe.

There was a microphone over my head and I screamed into it,
"Get me out of here! I can't breathe!" Immediately the technician
brought me out of the tunnel.

"Unstrap me, please unstrap me!" I pleaded. As she unstrapped
me, I sat up on the table, trembling. My eyes were wide with fear,
and I was straining for air.

"I was sexually abused as a child," I told her, "and sometimes I
can't breathe in tight places, but if you'll work with me, I'm sure I
can manage the test."

She looked a little apprehensive but said she would be glad to do
anything I needed.

I breathed a sigh of relief and told her, "I can't be strapped down.
I promise I will not move a muscle but you can't strap me down."

She said she had never done that before but she would try it.
Then I requested she give me some trial runs into the tunnel. I
asked her to put me into the tunnel for a moment and then bring me
immediately out. I went into the tunnel three times in this manner
and then I told her I thought I could stay in it this time.

I was right. I was able to stay in the tunnel for about 30 minutes.
I kept my eyes closed and visualized myself in the Virgin Islands.
I saw the blue water and the far horizon and I breathed the cool
sea breeze. Then the table holding me moved farther into the
tunnel. Obviously the tests required a different part of my back on
the screen. Again, I had trouble breathing. I tried very hard to get
back to the Virgin Islands but I was unsuccessful. I was starting to
sweat and panic.

"I can't breathe, quickly . . . quickly . . . I have to come out now!"

She pushed the button and as I was coming out I sat up, relieved
to be able to breath again. I let her know I could go back in but I
just needed a moment. She told me I had about 15 minutes more in
the test. As I went back into the tunnel I was proud of myself. I had
transformed my fear and had communicated what I needed in order
to finish the test. As I left the room that day, the technician told me
she had not expected me to finish the test. I just looked at her and
smiled, knowing inside I was able to do anything I decided to do.
For a while that day I cried heavy tears but I ended up feeling angry

again because I had to endure this kind of experience in my life. More layers of fear and anger . . .

The Internal Terrorizer

In the beginning of my Gestalt therapy I became aware of a great deal of confusing fear. It seemed I was generalizing the actual fear that was part of the rapes into areas of my life that were not necessarily fearful. My therapist called it "terrorizing"; she said that I was terrorizing myself. This terrorizer is part of the internalized abuser that I discuss in the chapter on victimization. The internalized terrorizer was the part of myself that kept fear in my life, that kept me scared. The event of the rape was long gone but I was keeping it going by keeping myself scared. Part of the reason I adopted the terrorizer as a part of my personality was that I felt somehow it was my fault I was raped and if I would just be on guard, not trusting events and people, then I would be safe. I could avoid being raped again if I would stay afraid, and so I stayed afraid.

Transformation is the key to fear. Just as the energy in oil is transformed into the energy of gasoline which has a different purpose, so can fear be transformed into a different energy which also has a different purpose.

> *Fear can be changed, fear can be transformed into love.*

The origin of fear is from the lower energy centers of the body and if it is not transformed into the higher energy center of the heart, it will continue to control at a base level. It will keep fear in your life and keep power out of your life.

The Meadow Exercise

Visualization during meditation is helpful for this transformation.

Lie down on something comfortable. Take a few deep breaths to help center your mind. Then imagine yourself in a beautiful meadow. All around you are yellow daffodils and yellow marigolds. Breathe in the fragrance of yellow. Visualize the yellow entering your nose and going down your throat and into your lungs. As it reaches your lungs it expands into your whole trunk and down into your genital area. You are already feeling more peaceful. As you continue breathing your entire body is filled with the fragrance of yellow. Now slowly go back to the meadow. There is someone waiting for you in the meadow. It is a deer. Stand in front of the deer and look into her eyes. What do you see? . . . Now very quickly step into the deer's body. What does it feel like to be inside the deer? . . . Look through the deer's eyes at the meadow . . . What do you see? . . . The world has changed, hasn't it? You are able to see the slightest movement in the distance and everything is crystal clear.

Now concentrate on the heart area of the deer . . . What do you feel now? . . . Warmth, a large warmth . . . Love . . . the deer has an enormous capacity for love. In a moment you are going to leave the deer's body but before you do, you can decide to take two things with you. You can take the vision of the deer . . . the ability to see the world in a different way . . . and you can take the energy of the heart of the deer . . . the deer's capacity for love. Thank the deer for its gifts.

You are once more standing in the meadow. In a moment you will be opening your eyes, and when you open your eyes, you will have three things, three gifts of transformation: new vision, a new capacity for love and the calming of the color yellow in your body. Thank the meadow for its gifts and open your eyes.

This is an example of how you can transform fear into love, how you can take an energy that is paralyzing and change it into an energy that is empowering. Physicists today are discovering that all we are is energy, no matter how small the system that they are studying, it moves and is energy. It follows, then, that the pain of incest is also an energy, whether we are talking about fear, anger, sadness or any other emotion that accompanies childhood sexual abuse. If the pain is energy, then it can be transformed into another energy. The pain of incest can be transformed into the empowering energy of love.

Trust Begins Within

Trust and fear . . . Fear and trust are not found together. When a person is fearful, trust disappears. To have relationships, to have enjoyment in life and to venture forth into life's challenges, trust must replace fear.

For a survivor, trust does not begin with other people. Trust has to be redeveloped within ourselves. First, we need to learn to trust ourselves, to know who we are and what we really want before we can learn to trust others. This inner trust comes when we learn to love our wounded child.

6

Living The Role
Of Victim

Dream

I am in a gymnasium with several men. On the floor is a large rectangular space marked off with masking tape. The area within the space is controlled electronically from a panel behind the curtains. The men are trying to get me to dance into that space and if they are able to control me into the space, I will disappear. I look to the right and see the control panel behind the curtains and think about going after the controls but I decide there are too many men and I do not even try.

The men dance me into the rectangle and I stand there petrified. I look down at my hands and they start disappearing. Then my hands and arms feel electrified and tingly and they also disappear. Then my whole body disappears. I awaken from the dream very frightened.

A few years ago I participated in a self-realization seminar. I had just quit a peer counseling group and was still very much in the pain of the rape and not effectively dealing with it. The seminar was engineered to push all your buttons and make you very uncomfortable in order for you to reach down within yourself to open up places never seen before. The weekends consisted of long hours of sitting without much food, rest or bathroom time.

On the second day of the training, after my tiredness was wearing down my defenses, I stood up and took the microphone. With tears streaming down my face I shared the humiliation of being raped and how painful my life was to me. To my surprise the leader did not respond with empathy toward me.

He told me, "Yes, it's too bad that you were raped but at this point in your life it is history. Nothing can be done about that now, and you're still choosing to be a victim of the rape. All this feeling sorry for yourself and crying isn't doing you any good. What are you going to do about the quality of your life?"

I looked at him astonished. I had never heard this before and I did not really know what he was talking about. There was a hush around the room. More people than just myself felt he was being cruel. After all, I was raped, I was in pain and now he is telling me the pain is my responsibility. It certainly did not feel like my responsibility. What I was hearing him say was that it was my fault but, in fact, he was not saying that at all. He was telling me that there is only one person in charge of my life and if I wanted a quality life, then it was up to me to stop feeling sorry for myself and to stop being a victim of the rape.

In actuality, what he told me was important but without the next three years of Gestalt therapy, the information he gave me would have been useless. I believe that being given knowledge in this manner without an opportunity to integrate it into your life is like telling a child to drive a car when she neither has the maturity nor the skills necessary for the task. However, even though the information was given to me in a disconnected form, I never forgot what the leader said. Three years later I recall looking back and saying, "Now I know what he was talking about. I have been victimizing myself."

Internalizing The Abuser

Until a person who has been sexually abused as a child acknowledges her pain and decides to let it go — to release it and heal it — she will be a victim of the rape and she will be her own worst enemy. She is not in control of her life, the rape is. The survivor who is in the victim stage is not aware she is victimizing herself. Often she will think that what she is doing is powerful but because the wounded child within her is not healed, the thing she thinks is powerful could possibly be a continuation of the abuse. She will make choices in her life that are not in her best interest. Her friends and family will not understand why she is making such terrible choices. Most of the time her choices will in some way keep the abuse going and will in some way put her down.

Do not underestimate the negative power of anger. At this stage in her growth the abused person is very angry. However, instead of using her anger to go within and heal herself, she is using it to take action in the world — but as her own abuser.

Whether the sexual abuse has been repeated over a period of time or occurred only once, the victim internalizes an abuser. This internalized abuser continues to abuse the survivor, reminding her that she did something wrong.

When the abuse happened at an early age before the personality was significantly developed, sometimes personalities split off and the victim, in order to survive, develops more than one personality. At least one of these personalities will be a very harsh abuser. Fortunately, this personality split does not happen to everyone. More often, a person who has been sexually abused as a child has just one personality but this personality carries with it an abusive element. The child within, the child who survived the rape, thought it was her fault and that she should be punished.

Continuation Of The Pain

How the survivor responds to this victim stage depends on many factors. How or what the survivor was taught about sexuality overall in her childhood affects how she will view herself in the world. How did her mother teach her by example about what it is to be a woman: Is a woman used by men sexually? Is sex a duty performed by wives in the darkness of the bedroom? Is her body the only asset a woman has?

My mother, through osmosis, taught me not to enjoy my body, that my asset was not my body but my brains. If my mother had been a different kind of woman, a woman who exploited her body, my victim role might have been very different. I have always played down my body and have emphasized my brains.

A possible area where people can get caught up in the victim/abuser role after sexual abuse is prostitution. Many people who go into prostitution were sexually abused as children. These people are still in the victim role, they are still functioning out of the pain of the rape. For a person sexually abused as a child to sell her body represents a continuation of the abuse. The cause of this could be the way she was raped, the result of being publicly ridiculed, or it could possibly be a combination of the unknowns of how she already had been treated by her family.

Very often men who rape children call them whores and sluts to alleviate their own guilt and to keep the child in submission. If that occurs often enough, then the survivor, having heard it frequently, might choose to make a living that way. Thus the abuse helps to create a self-fulfilling prophecy. The survivor feels she is somewhat in control but the truth is not enough healing has taken place for the person to stop victimizing herself. The survivor is hurting and is unaware that she is now continuing the pain herself.

Reacting To Disbelief

It can be very painful to tell people that you have been a victim of rape. If you are not at an advanced stage of healing, it can be very damaging if no one believes you. If you are publicly embarrassed and disbelieved it can be even more devastating for you.

There is a place in every raped person's mind that does not believe it happened either because it was too awful to believe. If a survivor shares with someone information about the rape, she will then find herself in a terrible psychological bind if they do not believe her while she herself is still in a place of nonbelief. This bind can result in the survivor making harmful choices she would not ordinarily make. There are other choices for these people, there are always choices as along as we are alive, but first comes understanding.

The Choices We Make

An example of continuing victimization for a woman survivor is how she chooses to dress. For instance, the woman may dress suggestively, unconsciously inviting more abuse. She may gain weight or wear clothes too big for her, unconsciously saying do not notice me. Both choices are still living in the victim role, because neither woman is choosing from a place of freedom about her body. Neither woman owns her body.

The woman who dresses suggestively has internalized the pain in such a way that she has decided to control men on her terms, fooling herself into thinking that she is calling the shots. She thinks that if she is the one who entices them this time, then she can win. The other woman who puts on 20 or more pounds and wears clothes too big also feels a certain amount of control. She usually thinks that if a man wants her, it will be for her true self, not for the sexual being which is very hard to find underneath all the fat and clothes.

Taking a job beneath your skills, not going back for a GED when you did not finish high school and remaining in an abusive relationship are some of the ways we continue to victimize ourselves. Sabotaging a goal before it is met, not demanding child support and blaming others are also part of victimization.

The Victim Dream

The dream at the beginning of this chapter occurred in the beginning of my Gestalt therapy. Even though the rape had occurred decades before, the dream was symbolically showing me that I was still being controlled by the abuse I had suffered and that I was now victimizing myself.

To look at the dream from a Gestalt point of view, each part of the dream is me. I am the gymnasium, the building that allows destruction within itself. I am also the men who are sadistically controlling me. I am the electronic grid which has the power to make me invisible and nonexistent. I am also the powerless and frightened woman. I am the curtains which veil my own power. The only part of the dream which has the power to stop the destruction is the control panel and that is out of reach behind the curtains. I am out of contact with the powerful part of myself.

This was a very difficult dream for me to look at and process. It took enormous courage to see the destructive elements of my own personality. At first, to begin to process this dream, I became the control panel to get in touch with my own power. When I was able to feel my own power I then needed to connect that power to the woman in the dream who was so powerless, who had allowed the men to control her so totally. I was then able to experience the more destructive parts of myself: the curtains which kept me from my own power, the controlling men, the destructive grid, the powerlessness of the woman and the building which allowed this destruction to take place within itself. (Please refer to the chapter "Windows to the Self" for more on dream analysis.)

By looking at my victimization through the lens of my own dream, I was able to integrate the destructive parts of my personality. Until I could own my destructive side I was not able to let it go. The dream allowed me to see my destructive side while at the same time enabling me to contact the part of myself that is powerful. If a therapist had simply told me of my destructive side, as the leader in the self-realization workshop did, it would have had very little impact on me. Because the dream came from my own subconscious, I was able to experience my victimization in a way that I had never been able to do before. It is very difficult to look at how we victimize ourselves and we truly need to be with trained therapists for this task.

The rape is where the damage was done. The rape is where the life force was weakened, where the personality took on different and sometimes defeating elements. It is time to start understanding ourselves for the choices we make after being raped. A raped person making poor choices is still in the victim role of her healing, and within her is a very wounded child.

Rape has a devastating effect on anyone, regardless of the age of the victim. As healing takes place the survivor can begin to peel off the layers of self-abuse.

Ending Victimization

A few years ago I attended a weekend workshop with Pat Rodegast. Pat channels a spiritual being named Emmanuel who shares a deep wisdom of both the universe and also of each individual person. I felt very fortunate attending the workshop because it was not large and each person was able to talk with both Emmanuel and with Pat.

As the workshop drew to a close, Emmanuel gave the participants one last assignment. We were to rewrite our history in any way we desired, then we each could read our new life story to the group and to Emmanuel. I took the assignment very seriously and I chose not to rewrite my life up to that point. I could not see the benefit of saying I was not raped because the fact was I had been. I decided to write my story five years into the future. I wrote my deepest desires concerning my life to be.

The following is my recollection of my story and of Emmanuel's reactions. The story went something like this: I am a successful author of several books, the most popular being the book on healing the wounded child of incest. I also have a degree in counseling, a successful counseling practice and I participate with other colleagues in giving workshops around the country. I feel quite beautiful and weigh a comfortable weight. My daughter is in a creative and performing arts college and I have a wonderful man in my life who is a partner, lover and friend.

As I finished reading the story, Emmanuel looked at me and asked me, "What will it cost you in your life to let this happen?"

I replied, "I will have to stop being a victim."

"Do you dare to let it be?" Emmanuel asked.

I answered, "Yes!"

7

Patterns
Of Survival

Dream

I was with a woman I had known in California. She seemed very distraught. Each night she felt afraid someone was going to rape her. She handled her fear by getting out of bed 20 minutes out of every hour to make certain she was safe. I asked her if there was not something better she could do, such as installing a burglar system. I asked, "Don't you know about sleep deprivation? It can make you crazy." I awakened very afraid.

Patterns of survival . . .

During times of crisis we choose ways of dealing with our families and our world that remain with us for the rest of our lives. These patterns of survival were necessary for us to get through the crisis in the first place and then to get through further hard times. Even though the patterns usually become obsolete as we get older and our needs change, they usually are not discarded without conscious choice and hard work.

A few months ago I began biofeedback to try to reduce my blood pressure without the use of drugs. The night before seeing the biofeedback therapist I had the dream at the beginning of this chapter. I had forgotten it, though, until I was in his office. As I was sharing with him a brief history of myself, the memory of the dream came over me. I decided to tell him about the dream.

As I related the dream to him, I also realized that symbolically, in my life, I get up 20 minutes out of every hour and that I am never relaxed. When he asked me the reason for this behavior, I realized it was because I was afraid that my daughter, not me, would be raped. Over the next few meetings I was able to piece together one of my patterns of survival.

A Childhood Promise

During these sessions with the therapist I also remembered another piece of my past. Part of this had always been a memory:

> *I am standing in front of the mirror in the bedroom of the house where my father raped me. I am crying but I am also strong and determined. I face myself in the mirror and make a promise to myself: "I promise myself I will*

never have a child, so the child will never hurt like this."
The next sentence I did not remember until I was 45: "I
promise never to have a child, to make certain no one ever
rapes a child of mine and makes my child hurt like this."

I made that promise to myself when the act of being raped by
my father was still part of my actual conscious memory. As an
adult I had known I did not want children but I was not consciously aware that I had made the promise to myself as a direct result
of having been raped. When I met the man I eventually married,
I was unaware of my hidden memories but I was very much aware
of not wanting children. It fit into what he wanted in the world,
too, and for the first two years of our marriage, having children
was not even discussed.

However, several of our friends starting having babies and somehow I forgot about my promise of many years before. Five months
into the pregnancy I developed high blood pressure. The doctors
called it idiopathic high blood pressure which means they did not
know why I had it. I was not overweight. I was not eating salty foods
or drinking caffeine. I was also not working which might have been
stressful. Toward the end of the pregnancy I developed toxemia and
the pregnancy ended with a C-section. Thankfully my daughter was
fine and healthy but I continued to have high blood pressure.

The Subconscious Mind

The subconscious mind is very literal. It can be likened to very
rich soil which will grow any seed planted. The seed I planted so
strongly that day in front of the mirror was that: I will never have a
child so no one will rape her.

The hypnotist I went to several years ago told me the subconscious mind takes that promise and says, "If that is so, then if I have
a child, she will be raped."

I did have a child. My child was a girl, and I have not been able
to relax since.

It was time to give my subconscious mind a different message. I
decided to erase the original. I pictured the original message in front
of me on a piece of paper, and I visualized the words disappearing.
Then, in its place, I wrote:

It is safe to have a child.
My daughter is safe.

It is safe to have a child.
My daughter is safe.
It is safe to have a child.
My daughter is safe.

Repetition

Over and over and over again! I am even now continuing to say it because the subconscious mind needs the constant repetition in order to erase a negative pattern that has previously been repeated so often.

The truth is my daughter is safe. There is no one in her life who would harm her and I feel she has learned to use good judgment in trusting people. Therefore, I know I can relax and release an old pattern of survival.

Another pattern I have remembered promising myself in that house is: "I don't need anybody. I can take care of myself."

As patterns go, it is not a bad pattern to have in order to survive in the world. With this pattern I graduated from college and have supported myself. Since my divorce I have started my own private practice and it has been successful. However, since I am now not in the crisis of the rape and am trying to live with my family of origin, the pattern is now creating the wrong direction for me in my life. For the most part, I am alone. I have discovered I do need people and I do want people to take care of me from time to time.

I have also chosen to erase this pattern from my subconscious and have replaced it with:

I want people in my life.
I accept help in my life.
I want people in my life.
I accept people in my life.
I want people in my life.
I accept people in my life.

Over and over and over again. One of Newton's laws of motion states that a moving object continues in the same path unless a force from outside the path pushes it off its path. There is energy holding us on to the paths we take, and unless we use more energy of a different kind, we will not be able to get ourselves off the path. I believe this to be so even if the path or pattern is no longer in our best interest. Change is difficult. It is much easier to stay in the same old rut but it has been my experience that once you actually choose the path of change, it does eventually get easier. The most difficult step is initially taking a new direction. However, after the first few changes it no longer feels as if you are walking through mud and mire. I believe the reason I have tried different kinds of healing has been because old patterns die hard. Sometimes I have needed a new approach, a new energy.

Healing In Layers

Many years ago someone told me that healing occurs in layers, like peeling an onion. The outside layers are thicker than the inside layers, and they are also bigger. As you get to the inside of the onion, it gets easier to peel: The layers are thinner and smaller. I also believe that another way healing is like an onion is the tears that need to be shed. Tears are healing. If a person who has been abused sexually as a child is going to heal herself, then she must expect to cry a great deal.

At the last Gestalt workshop I attended, a woman who had known me for several years came to me and said, "I don't want you in my life, Mary, because you're sad all the time."

I was furious. I went there expecting to work. While there, I *was* sad a great deal of the time because there were many layers of sadness which were involved in peeling the onion of my childhood sexual abuse. She was upset with me because, although she felt her brand of suffering was just as bad as mine, she did not feel sad all the time.

Healing Yourself

If a person is going to heal herself, then she has to decide to heal herself regardless of the opinions of friends and relatives. The road to healing is a difficult one, and although I have found some short-cuts in the last two years, it is still a long road. From my experience, both in healing myself and in observing other people heal, I have strongly concluded that you cannot compare one person's process with the process of another. Each of us has had a different childhood and the path to wholeness is not the same for everyone. We need to surround ourselves with loving, generous people and if you can only find one of those in your world, then keep just that one around.

Judge carefully the friends you keep. Make certain they are not continuing to abuse you. The pattern I am still working on concerning people in my life will work only if I learn to exercise discerning judgment on how to pick people whose hearts are intact, people who will add to my life, not detract from it. As we are changing these patterns of survival, we must also learn new lifeskills that support the new patterns to eliminate getting whopped in the head again.

I developed my pattern that I do not need anybody because the people who were in my life when I was a child were not trustworthy. If I work to change the pattern to say that now I accept help in my life and that I want people in my life — and if I do not at the same time change my standards of choosing my friends — then I am going to continue to have people in my life who are not trustworthy and I will be abusing myself again.

The Upward Spiral Of Growth

A therapist once told me that another way to look at the growth process is to use the analogy of an upward spiral. Often, while I have been healing myself, I have met head-on with what felt to me to be the same situation again. After looking at the issues I began to realize it was the same piece of garbage but I also realized that I was looking at it from a different point of view.

Imagine a spiral in front of you, like a Slinky pulled apart and held vertically. On one side of the spiral is sadness. Two years ago you were on the fourth upward turn and while you were there, you were very sad. Now, two years later, you begin to feel sad again. It starts to feel to you as though you have not achieved anything in the past two years, making you even sadder.

The difference, however, is that you are now on the seventh upward turn, and you are, in fact, nowhere near where you were two years ago. It only feels the same. It is not the same, not at all. If you can see your growth from this perspective, you will not fall down in the mud and mire again. What you will experience is another segment of sadness that has to be released and let go. You will find your growth moving faster.

A great deal of pain can be avoided when you understand you really are not in the same place but it only *feels* that way. Then, in two more years when you hit sadness again, you will say to yourself, "This is a different experience from the last time. I'm not as sad and it is only lasting a day instead of a month." This is the upward spiral of growth. Energy moves in spirals. The truth is we are never the same from moment to moment and if we can incorporate that idea into our growth, we will not have as many down times. Those that we do have will be shorter.

Examples Of Negative Patterns

The following are examples of patterns that a survivor might possibly experience from various encounters of childhood sexual abuse. We can now see how they need to be changed consciously for our lives to improve:

> *I can't trust anybody.*
> *I've already been exploited, I might as well exploit myself.*
> *Life is hard, and you don't get anywhere.*
> *I'm not pretty.*
> *It doesn't matter what I do with my body now.*
> *If I'm fat and ugly, I'll never be raped again.*
> *He said I'm a whore, so I might as well be one.*
> *I'll never be a man now. (For survivors of boyhood rape.)*
> *I can never tell anyone about this.*

Positive Affirmations

Patterns of survival can be changed. Make the negative statement into a positive statement. Then use it as an affirmation that you repeat over and over again.

> *I pick trustworthy people.*
>
> *I'm a worthwhile person and I deserve the best.*
>
> *Life is easy and I can accomplish anything.*
>
> *I'm beautiful.*
>
> *My body is beautiful and I choose who touches it.*
>
> *It's safe for me to be thin and beautiful.*
>
> *I'm a beautiful human being and I believe in myself.*
>
> *I am strong and admired.*
>
> *I have the strength to share my pain.*

These are examples of positive patterns. Because each person's life is different, the patterns also will be different. Discover your patterns and change them. Your life will be different. Having a different life can be felt as frightening. Learn to release the fear and you will find that you can then take one step after another toward wholeness.

8

Thoughts Of Suicide

Dream

I was in the back seat of a black limousine. I had been asleep and as I awakened, I noticed the chauffeur was dressed in black. There was a person next to him in the front seat. I could tell it was a woman and at first I thought it was a friend of mine. Then the figure reminded me of my mother, who was dead.

I called to her, "Mom?" The feminine figure in the front seat kept her face veiled and reached into the back seat with her hand gloved in black past her elbow. As she reached into the back seat, she said, "Just rest for now." The chauffeur then said, "We are backing up here to wait for the others to catch up." Then I noticed the limousine was backing up onto a little-used grassy road. I could see the cars going by on the highway. I looked out the window and saw a row of trees on each side of the car. Behind the green trees were large oil refinery storage tanks.

Without darkness there would not be light, without night there would not be day and without death there would not be life. That is the balance of the universe. For one thing to exist, its opposite must exist — the yin and yang of life. Without winter, without a time of rest, summer would not be as bountiful. Without the rhythm of opposites, life could not continue.

In a person sexually abused as a child, who has not healed the wounded child within her, there can be an imbalance, there can be more darkness than light. The natural yin/yang balance is disrupted. There is a tendency toward darkness, toward the dark side of life. In this state of darkness it is easy for the survivor to contemplate suicide, to want to kill the physical body through which she has felt so much pain.

Seeking The Light

One of my teachers, Twylah Nitsch, a Seneca Indian elder, told me that the color black is not a negative color in her culture. The color black means "seeking the light." This approach to the color black and to the darkness of the universe touched my heart deeply. If the person who has been sexually abused as a child can see her own darkness as "seeking the light," as going toward enlightenment, then the act of suicide should never be a reality for her. She simply will look at her darkness, her depression, her desire to be dead, as a road to knowledge, as a way back to her true self, as a path to the light.

It is important to distinguish between thoughts of suicide and the actual act of killing the physical body. The actual act of suicide should never happen. It is a misinterpretation of the darkness. In a person who has been sexually abused as a child, a disintegration of the personality occurs. For the personality to become whole again it is necessary to look at the darkness, to face the pain.

Thoughts of suicide are the attempt of the personality to come to wholeness, to once again integrate the personality. Thoughts of suicide well up from the depths of the damaged person in order to alert that person that there is a darkness within that must be looked at and brought into balance.

The darkness has a wisdom within itself if the survivor is able to see it. I remember a song from my childhood called *The Hanging Tree*. It was sung by Marty Robbins. I do not remember all the words but one of the lines went like this: "To really live you must almost die."

To almost die is an act of transformation; it is one of the most courageous acts a human being can accomplish: it is the courage of the inner journey of transformation of darkness into light, transformation of death into life, and transformation of pain into joy.

To walk into darkness purposefully has been the act of a warrior from the beginning of time. Medicine men and women have to descend into darkness before they can know the wisdom of the Great Mystery. They have to know their own fears, their own death before they can be vessels of true knowledge.

In looking at thoughts of suicide, the true question is: death of what? It is not death of the physical self; it is death of the past, death of the pain, the death of the part of us that is the victim. The death of the self-hatred is the transformational goal of the journey into darkness.

Rage

Suicide also carries with it rage and an act of revenge and punishment for the loved ones whom we feel have not loved and supported us. Unexpressed anger and rage can be turned inward toward ourselves instead of expressing it outwardly where it belongs. "They'll be sorry when I'm gone. Then they'll know how badly they have hurt me." Never allow yourself to buy into this trick of the darkness. Never turn that rage inward toward yourself. Make certain you have a therapist who can help you handle anger and express it. It was *never* our fault we were raped and it is time we stopped punishing ourselves. At one point in my therapy I consciously worked in my everyday life to put the anger where it belonged. I gave myself permission to tell people when they were treating me wrongly, even if the way I told them was done badly. I decided that done badly was better than not being done at all. As survivors of childhood sexual abuse, we think every problem is our fault and we have to learn carefully which garbage is ours and which belongs to someone else.

It is true that in our childhoods we were not properly supported but killing ourselves for revenge on those people is in effect joining them in saying we are worthless. We would be choosing to walk across an invisible line: the line that separates who we really are from who our oppressors have taught us to be. By killing ourselves we would be abandoning our wounded child totally and agreeing with our oppressors.

When suicidal thoughts arise, there is also an underlying desire to go home again in order to have total peace, security and protection. The survivor of childhood sexual abuse has a deep need for comfort and it is sometimes tempting for the survivor to fool herself into thinking that if she is dead, she will be comforted. It is a mistake to think along these lines — death by suicide is not a comfort.

> *Years ago when I was a Zen student, the Zen master told me the following:*
> *There is an ancient Zen story about a Zen master who is teaching a student. The Zen master asks the student how great his desire to learn is, and the student replies that it is great. The Zen master then takes his student to a river, pushes his head under the water and holds it there. Just before the student has run out of air, the master releases his hold on the student's head. The student gasps for air with all of his being. The Zen master then tells him: That's how much your desire needs to be. You need to want it more than anything else in the world.*

The Shadow Of Death

This should also be the situation with the survivor of incest. She needs to want to heal herself more than anything else in the world. She needs to be willing to walk "through the valley of the shadow of death." The key word in this *23rd Psalm* is *shadow*. It is not death we are facing, it is the shadow of death. It is the place where we integrate our pain and our hurts. Just as our shadow is not us, neither is the shadow of death actual death. Being in the shadow of death leads to life. Being in the shadow of death leads to light and the integration of our personality.

By walking through the valley of the shadow of death you can learn of the transformative quality that death teaches. Death is about change of form, change of energy. By being in its shadow we can learn its lessons of transformation without experiencing physical death.

Clairvoyant people and psychics travel into the shadow of the future. They are not actually in the future, they are in its shadows, shadows of what might be.

Control

I believe that the thought of suicide for the survivor of rape is, at least in part, a matter of attempt at control, a matter of power for people who have experienced the deepest level of powerlessness. Part of the picture for me was an agreement I made with myself after I was raped, an agreement that I could always escape by killing myself if things got too tough. During the rape I did not have an out, and so I gave myself an out for the rest of my life — seemingly, a last act of power. In the end I am in control and I have the final say. This is again, however, one of the tricks of darkness.

If I cannot have power over my life, then I will have power over my death. This, however, is the terrible deception that darkness can weave: Suicide is not an act of power, suicide is the final act of powerlessness. The darkness has tried to deceive us — if we cannot learn to take power in our world, then killing ourselves is also a lack of power. Darkness without knowledge can trick you and make you think physical death is an act of power. The comfort we desperately seek is not on the other side. The comfort we desperately seek is within us. The only comfort that counts is the comfort we carefully learn to give ourselves. Our true power lies within, our true power lies in our own ability to love ourselves.

A Transformation

Recently I went through a deep transformative process. The dream at the beginning of this chapter predicted both the darkness and the ensuing transformation.

The dream occurred about two weeks after I discovered a second herniated disc in my back. The neurosurgeon told me I could not return to my current profession and that I needed surgery again. As a single parent whose only source of income was as a practicing physical therapist, I was in shock. A key to the depths of darkness I descended into over the next few weeks is that in a life of pain and heartache as a survivor of incest, I had always felt powerful in my work as a pediatric physical therapist. I enjoyed what I did and I could make a comfortable living for myself and my daughter. To now have my job taken from me left me feeling more powerless than I had ever felt in my adult life.

Another incident compounded the powerlessness the day the dream occurred. The man I had been in love with for two years pulled away and did not want to be my lover anymore. In addition to this loss, the pain from the herniated disc became unbearable. The pain went down my leg and I began to lose the function of my foot muscles.

My friends also dropped away and I was alone with my pain and my feeling of powerlessness in the world. It was, without a doubt, the most intense learning experience I have ever encountered.

Wanting to die became an obsession with me. I thought about it day and night. I wanted the pain to go away — I just wanted the pain to go away, both physical and psychological.

I was in the darkness again, the darkness originally created by the childhood rapes. Only this time it was different. I saw no way out of my pain. I had no money, I had no job, I seemingly had no friends and I was in constant physical pain. I could not even tie my own shoes.

Synchronicity

After a few days of being in this enormous darkness, I found myself in a video store. I had the sense that I was looking for something special but I did not know what. My eyes caught a movie title, *Orpheus.* For no reason obvious to me, I picked it out and took it home. At the time I did not remember Orpheus was from Greek mythology and that he was prematurely taken to the other side by death.

The movie, made in 1949, was in black and white. *Orpheus* was made in France and subtitled in English. As I watched the movie I found my hair begin to stand on end. Orpheus was a poet who was in love with his lovely wife. He was in a local cafe when Death came to town in a black limousine driven by a chauffeur. Death was a woman dressed in black and she sat in the front seat with the chauffeur. This feminine Death had been sent to town from "the other side" to take a young man having a drink at the cafe to his death. However, when Death saw Orpheus, she fell in love with him and asked him to get in the back seat of the limousine.

Death, because of her love for Orpheus, decided she would take Orpheus' wife and then Orpheus to the other side. These were not her orders and it resulted in a premature death for both Orpheus and his wife. When Death took the wife, Death put on black gloves that extended up past her elbow. After she finally took Orpheus and his wife to the other side, she began to experience emotions she did not ordinarily have. She then decided she had done a terrible thing and, even though she knew she would be punished in the underworld, she gave Orpheus and his wife back their lives.

I found the scenes in the underworld exciting to watch. When Death gave Orpheus back his life, she told him to walk backwards through time in order that what had been would not be! The chauffeur took the hand of Orpheus and they both walked backwards. They walked against a strong, forceful wind. With a great deal of effort Orpheus found himself back in his bedroom with his wife, lying on the bed. What had been, had been erased. He once again felt himself in love with his wife and although Orpheus remembered his journey into darkness, his wife remembered nothing.

As I watched the movie unfold, I could barely breathe. The black limousine, the chauffeur, the feminine Death with black gloves past her elbow were directly from my dream! I found that the synchronicity of dreaming my dream and of selecting this movie I had never noticed before — a movie that contained so many of the symbols of my own dream — resulted in opening my consciousness. I began to see my own journey into darkness as a journey I had to take in order to have a different life, a journey of healing.

I saw Orpheus' encounter with Death as a journey within. A journey into his own darkness to integrate the unknown parts of his personality, culminating in his journey toward wholeness. Orpheus not only had to go into his darkness, but also he had to come back to the present time to integrate what he had learned into his real life. The internal learning does not work unless it is integrated into our everyday life.

The Feminine Death

Carl Jung, the noted psychologist, wrote that the feminine death in dreams is about transformation and is not a warning about a physical death. The death figure in my dream and the death figure in *Orpheus* were both feminine. Feminine energy is about renewal and rebirth. It follows that a feminine death is a positive dream symbol. The feminine death in my dream was taking me into my darkness but not to die a physical death. She was taking me into my darkness to be reborn, to be transformed. A new me was about to be born of the feminine transformative side of myself. A new me! I was about to become a whole woman: a woman who loves herself, a woman who sees her vision and activates her dreams in the world.

My old self had to die in order for a new life to unfold. I was standing on a threshold of new beginnings that was of such magnitude I had to say goodbye to an entire way of life — my job which did not meet my needs anymore, friends who were not capable of loving the new me and an old physical self that tended toward sickness. In truth, "to really live, you must almost die."

A clue in my dreams of the ensuing transformation was the large storage tanks filled with black oil. The blackness was no longer in the bowels of the earth. It had been extracted and was waiting in storage tanks to be transformed into another form of energy. This black oil symbolized my own darkness within my personality. The darkness was no longer within me; it was just waiting for me to see my power in the world and to transform it from darkness into light. The green trees held the promise of growth and renewal and also formed a protective guard over me — already within me were sturdy, green, growing trees of love standing guard over me, over my journey into darkness.

Another important symbol that occurred both in my dream and in *Orpheus* was the movement backwards. In my dream the black limousine was backing up to wait for the others to catch up and in *Orpheus,* the feminine Death who gave Orpheus back his life told him to walk backwards in order that what had been will not be. Lost time was implied in my dream. If the others had to catch up, then I was ahead of them; I was backing up while they were coming forward. For Orpheus to regain his life he had to walk backwards through time. For me to regain my life, I also had to walk backward through time in order that what had been would not be.

The Wounded Child

If every symbol in the dream is me, then part of me is in one place in time and another part of me is in another place in time. The wounded child within me is still stuck in time 40 years ago. Other parts of my personality grew and matured and functioned well in the world; they went forward in time. However, my inner child who was so brutally raped at five and who was not comforted in any way at all except with a bag of candy, that child is alive inside of me but time for her is 40 years ago. Time does not move forward for her. She is always five years old, it is always 1948 and she is always in pain. She always wants candy when she feels badly, she never feels comfortable around people, she does not trust anyone and when the real world becomes scary, threatening and precarious, she wants to die.

It is the wounded child within us who wants to die. Most of the time we do not function out of our inner wound, our inner wounded child. Most of the time we function out of the mature adult who goes to work, takes care of the family and sees to everyday activities. However, when external events are so similar to the original wound, then the wounded child dominates our personality and the wish to die dominates our thoughts. The two external events that trigger me are powerlessness and humiliation. Usually when they come together, I am thrown back into the darkness again.

The aim of the darkness, the transformative goal of the darkness, is to get us to look again at our inner child who is so wounded that she desires to die. Healing our inner wounded child is the one most important thing we can do for ourselves as survivors of childhood sexual abuse.

It is not the external circumstances that are making the survivor want to kill herself; it is her internal darkness, her wounded child. The desire to die is a direct result of the rape which weakened our life force and only by facing the inner darkness and healing the wounded child can the survivor of childhood sexual abuse be whole. When the wounded child is healed, the survivor will no longer be plagued by thoughts of suicide when external events attempt to make her powerless.

The Act Of Power

It is of considerable importance to realize that for healing to occur, for the wounded child to be acknowledged and healed, for the person sexually abused as a child not to kill herself, she has to *decide* not to kill herself. In the journey into darkness there is a point of transformation, there is a point where the person turns around and goes toward the light. This point of transformation comes when she decides not to kill herself. With this decision not to die, she has found lessons in the darkness. Without this decision not to die, the darkness just remains darkness with all its pitfalls, fear and illusions and does not lead to the light. The decision not to die is the survivor's true act of power.

The decision not to kill yourself is essential to the process of looking at the darkness. In the healing of your wounded child it is pivotal to decide not to die. How that decision is made is different for each person but certainly seeing your life in the larger picture of the journey of the soul toward the light can give you the perspective to make the decision to live. After you have made the decision to live, follow it up with *millions* of affirmations choosing life — over and over again.

The jewel of light at the end of your journey into darkness is that you are in charge of your life, you are in charge of your healing. This is your true power, to choose to live, to choose life. As soon as you truly choose to live, answers will come to you and you will be in the rhythm of life again. You never received what you needed as a child, and now the secret to healing, the secret to healing your inner wounded child, is that you are now the only person who can give that much needed love to yourself. You are your own true healer of the darkness. That is the power of the darkness. That is its hidden wisdom.

PART TWO

The Journey
Into Light:
More Ways To Heal

9

Tools To Release Thoughts Of Suicide

Visualization: Imagine yourself with both hands over your ears and standing in the center of an oak tree. Breathe deeply in and out. Feel your feet snuggle into the roots of the tree and your legs and back become like the trunk of the tree. Your arms become the branches and your hands become the leaves that blow gently in the breeze. Remember to give thanks for oak trees that give strength and air to breathe.

Rainbow Dancer
by Melinda Joy Miller
and Jane Rachfalski

A person needs tools and equipment to go on a journey and it is important to have the proper equipment for a safe journey. Before you can turn and look at the darkness on your journey toward wholeness, you have to make certain you are strong enough to survive the trip.

Proper nourishment is essential if you are dealing with thoughts of suicide. If you are unable to eat or if you are only eating sugar and junk foods, then your judgment may be clouded. If you turn toward your darkness with clouded judgment, it is too easy to mistake the darkness for power and to end up killing your physical self.

In childhood sexual abuse, the life force has been damaged, the will to live has been changed. If a person is considering suicide, the will to live is weak. Very often if the will to live is weak, eating habits are poor.

Color Healing

I have recently explored healing earth energies, and I have found them to be very helpful in preparing the body and the mind to go into the darkness. I have found the earth energy of color to be very effective in healing myself of the pain of childhood sexual abuse.

Color is light. Light originates in the fiery energy of the sun. The sun's light is pure energy. Our bodies are made of moving energy. This moving energy has color. Healers from the East have recognized for thousands of years that the human body has centers of energy with corresponding colors and that these centers of energy keep the body and mind healthy. The colors of our chakras, as the energy centers are called, are the colors of the rainbow. There are many people who are able to see this moving energy and its color; they are able to see people's auras.

Have you ever looked through a prism? A prism takes the light of the sun and breaks it down into its basic colors. The naked eye cannot see these colors without the prism but they are there, nonetheless. A prism helps us see the colors of the sun. People can also learn to see the colors of our energy centers.

I am writing this chapter in the middle of a Pennsylvania winter. It is January and there is a layer of about five inches of snow on the ground. It snowed yesterday but thick, gray clouds still hang over the landscape. There is no color anywhere. Gray penetrates every building and space. If people stay outside very long in this gray, it will penetrate them also. Many people become depressed in the winter months from the lack of color in their lives. The sun is our source of life-giving energy and of life-giving color.

Life Force And Color

The first color that comes to mind to help increase the will to live is red. Red is full of life-giving energy. However, because red activates the adrenals, I do not recommend it for survivors of childhood sexual abuse. Survivors live with a great deal of fear and already overuse their adrenal system. The adrenal glands are part of the sympathetic nervous system and gear the body for fear, fright or flight.

A more effective color for increasing our life force, our will to live, is orange. Orange is composed of red and yellow. With the use of orange the benefits of red will be absorbed into the body without the harmful stress on the adrenals. Orange is energy, it is strength. It is the warmth of the sun on a summer's day. Courage, stability and willpower are the constant companions of orange.

I apply the colors of the rainbow with a color lamp which can be purchased at Light Works & Co. (You will find its address in the accompanying appendix.) The lamp uses color gels and comes with a booklet on the benefits of color. I suggest that when using the lamp, you hang it on a hook over your bed or place it on a table next to your bed so that it shines down on you.

To strengthen your willpower, your will to live, put the orange colored gel into the lamp and bathe the room in orange for a while before the treatment. Make certain the room is warm because the color absorbs faster into the body when the body is bare. First, lie down on your stomach with the light shining on your feet and legs. After a few minutes adjust the light onto your thighs, buttocks and lower back. After about ten minutes turn onto your back and let the strengthening power of the sun enter your body just below your belly button. Adding a visualization is helpful during the treatment. Saying a life-affirming affirmation strengthens the power of the color of orange in your body. *"I choose life"* is a good affirmation. Change the wording to suit your personality. *"I choose to live"* or *"I love myself and I choose to live"* are possibilities.

A Color Visualization

Visualizing yourself lying on a beautiful white sandy beach with soft blue water lapping on the sand can be helpful. See yourself lying safely on the beach and imagine the warm orange sun entering your body just below your belly button. As it enters your body try to warm the area physically just below your belly button. When you begin to feel a warmth, allow it to enlarge until it fills your entire belly and flows down into your legs. Then allow the strong orange color to fill your chest and neck and head so that every cell in your body has renewed energy. End the visualization with a positive affirmation, affirming how wonderful you are and that you choose to live.

End the treatment with a vigorous shower. After you wet your body thoroughly with water, stand away from the water and rub sea salt briskly all over your body. Because your body is wet, the rubbing will be an awakening, not an abrasive feeling. When I was in physical therapy school, we learned this technique. It is called a salt glow. Combining the orange light and the salt rub will help your inner light to glow.

Top off the glow with nourishing food. An orange or a bowl of hearty soup might sound good. If you have a very weak life force, you will want to repeat this treatment daily until you are eating regularly. Sometimes thoughts of suicide can be due entirely to poor nutrition.

Menstruation And Depression

I also want to emphasize the importance of understanding our bodies and our cycles of menstruation. Years ago I read *Let's Get Well* by Adelle Davis. She said there is a physiological reaction in the body of a woman during menstruation that lowers the calcium level. She also stated that if the calcium level fell low enough, then thoughts of worthlessness and depression could develop. She discussed the effects of low calcium levels in the menstrual cycle and gave nutritional advice for women during this monthly cycle.

Occasionally I have experienced the feeling of worthlessness the day before menstruation and it will frequently continue for several days. I now take a calcium/magnesium tablet during that time and

I no longer experience those feelings. As survivors of childhood sexual abuse, both our bodies and minds were affected by the abuse. In taking our journey toward wholeness, our whole self needs to be considered.

The Sexual Energy Exercise

While working on the will to live, I tried an exercise a therapist had shared with me a few years before. Although the technique actually was for a different purpose, I changed it to meet my needs. The energy of the genital area is very powerful and can be used to create more than just babies. The energy of the genital area can also be moved up to higher chakras to fuel other parts of our bodies.

This exercise is designed to move the powerful energy of the genital area into the heart area. It is based on the belief that if we love ourselves, we cannot kill ourselves. This exercise is a very private and loving one toward yourself. You will be masturbating yourself into an orgasm, which I think of as an exercise in loving yourself. Again, using the color lamp is helpful. Bathe the room in orange because orange is the color of the second chakra which is the sexual chakra.

Before you begin loving yourself, have the green colored gel available. Begin loving yourself in any way you choose and, as you reach orgasm, take your hands and make sweeping strokes from your genital area up to your heart. Make the strokes rhythmical and say to yourself, "I love and believe in myself." Visually guide the sensual energy into your heart area.

Continue the strokes and the affirmation until the sensual feelings have left your body. Then slowly put the green gel into the color lamp, lie back and quietly continue the affirmations. Green is the color of the heart chakra and will help bring love into your heart. You may go to sleep. The rest will renew your spirit. Make certain that the lamp is in a safe place so you can really relax in the love of the green light. Green is the one color you cannot overdo. Repeat this exercise as often as you desire; survivors of childhood sexual abuse need as many loving sexual experiences as possible.

Music And The Life Force

I have also found the use of music to be extremely helpful. The use of my life song (refer to the chapter on healing sounds) has proven very important to me in my attempt to increase my life force on my journey toward wholeness. I have played it on the synthesizer and have recorded it with my voice over it, saying my own affirmations and my own life dreams. Hearing my own voice on my tape recorder with my life song in the background reaches deep within me and has helped to heal my wounded child.

Two other pieces of music have also been important to me to increase my will to live. I have taped the "Ode to Joy" section of Beethoven's Ninth Symphony over and over so I could listen to it. It is truly about joy! Also, Stevie Wonder has a song about hope that is unsurpassed, *A Place in the Sun*. Indeed, there is a place in the sun for us. We are truly worthwhile people. Music is a true gift and is a true healer.

Additionally, Melinda Miller, co-author of *Rainbow Dancer*, has taught me that a drum beat activates the first chakra and helps increase the life force.

Sleep

Another area in the survivor's life that can interfere with having sufficient strength to take the journey into darkness is sleep or the lack of it. Often when someone is dealing with thoughts of suicide, the anxiety becomes so great that sleep becomes erratic or nonexistent. There have been numerous scientific studies concerning the effects of lack of sleep on the personality and certainly if a person dealing with thoughts of suicide also is not sleeping well, that person's judgment is clouded.

Color therapy can be an aide in helping a person relax and sleep. The color indigo blue has very soothing energy. It is the color of the sixth chakra, commonly called the third eye, and is located just above the eyebrows. To calm yourself and to feel safe enough to sleep, I recommend a self-hypnosis tape from the Dick Sutphen organization called *Peaceful Sleep Programming*. I recommend making your room comfortable and pleasing, filled with the indigo blue light. Using a tape recorder with earphones, listen to Dick's soothing voice and let your conscious mind go on vacation.

Indigo blue takes away negativity and fear. Fear is the basis of anxiety and the color indigo blue is ideal for helping you to sleep. (Caution: The color light blue, for the throat chakra, also calms but because it can depress a person, I do not recommend it for people dealing with thoughts of suicide.)

An exercise from *Rainbow Dancer* is also helpful for bringing peaceful sleep. It is called "Sweet Dreams." Before going to sleep, cross your left ankle over your right ankle. Cross your arms at your heart. While clasping fingers, imagine that you are drifting on a little cloud in the light blue of the big blue sky. Below, gentle waves lull you to sleep. Say thank you to the blue sky and the gentle ocean waves.

If you find you are still facing anxiety after following these suggestions, you might also want to try finding tapes you can walk around listening to several times during the day. Some of the New Age music tapes are very relaxing and Dick Sutphen has distributed some of this music with subliminal suggestions in the background. Louise Hay, who wrote *You Can Heal Your Life,* has some wonderful tapes available for counteracting the negative messages we are constantly giving ourselves.

Friends

The last area you should look at before you turn toward the darkness concerns your friends. We were alone when we were raped and, in the deep pain of thoughts of suicide, being alone is sometimes enough to make a person give up. There is no specific color for friends but experiment with color in your wardrobe. Add some oranges and greens and yellows with a dash of purple. It might change how you feel about yourself as well as be interesting to other people. If there is not a friend in your life you can truly depend on, it is essential for you to have a therapist who can be called day or night. For anyone dealing with thoughts of suicide, working with a trained therapist is a must.

Friends often can be a significant problem for survivors of childhood sexual abuse as a result of how different we felt after the rape. Our awkwardness socially often can make it difficult to have friends. As part of our patterns we also often pick people for friends who let us down. What worse time could they pick to let us down than in a crisis of thoughts of suicide?

To help change the pattern of attracting trustworthy people in your life, please refer to the chapter on patterns of survival. These new affirmations need to be as important to you as your meals. Say them on the bus, walking the dog, doing housework, anytime, anyplace. You will be surprised how often you say negative thoughts to yourself.

Healing Earth Energies

Also, the truth about being alone is that we are never alone. Even if you do not believe in a God of any kind, if you will start exploring the healing earth energies, you will begin to be in touch with the

powerful energy of Mother Earth, the oak tree, the ocean, the moon,
the sun, the exquisitely beautiful flowers, the wind, the stars and the
fruits of the earth. You will gradually begin to understand that, indeed,
we are connected to everything on this planet. Hug an oak tree or
visualize yourself inside an oak tree and start to feel its power.

Begin to take a walk each evening and watch the moon and her
cycles. See how easily she goes from darkness into light. Appreciate
her ability to change and then give thanks to yourself for your
ability to change. We have been hurt by people and, sometimes,
when we are on this journey into light, we can feel safer with a tree
or the dependable sun than with human beings. When you are
hurting and feeling alone, when you want to die because you think
no one loves you, let the healing earth energies teach you that,
indeed, you are never alone.

Energy Follows Thought

The negative thoughts of "I want to die, I hate myself, I'm ugly,
I won't make it this time, I'll never change," carry energy with them.
If everything is energy, then thoughts are energy too. If a person is
dealing with thoughts of suicide and that person continues to in-
dulge in the thoughts and does nothing about ending them, then it
eventually will become very difficult for that person to do anything
constructive about those thoughts. That person will become hardened in their point of view, and only negativity will be possible in
their life. It is important to get through this stage of growth quickly
because the more you think about killing yourself, the more you *will*
think about killing yourself! Many of my teachers have taught me
that energy follows thought and the more energy you put into negativity, the more negativity you will have in your life. Change what
your mind is thinking and your life will change.

10

Dreams:
Windows To
The Self

Dream

I was at a crossroads, and there was a man to my right. I said to him, "I may never see you again because we both have different things to do. I have never been in this place before, but I will be safe because I have a map." I then looked to my left and there were roads laid out in rectangular patterns. Beyond the roads was a mountain range.

Three months later — another dream: I am at the same cross-roads looking at the same pattern of roads underneath the distant mountains. As I'm looking at the roads, they rise up into the sky and become windows in the sky! The windows are the turquoise hue of the New Mexico sky. I stare at the windows and then I awaken.

Dreams are windows to the self, to our hidden wholeness, to that place within each of us that holds our seeds of growth. These windows, these dreams, hold the secrets of our unfolding and by understanding our dreams, we are on the road to becoming whole.

The dream-maker within each of us wants to be recognized. If the dream-maker is listened to, more dreams, more visions of who we really are, will be given to us. By tapping into the enormous information of our dream world, we are tapping into the river of life, we are tapping into the depths of who we can potentially become.

Dreams come to us when we are asleep, when the ego is disconnected and not on guard. Thus a different kind of information is available to us in our dreams from that we receive in our waking times. The images of dreams have no limitations; lions can talk and people can fly. It is through the symbols of dreamtime that a person can catch glimpses of an inner world which cannot exist in our world of gravity and physical laws. It is really quite beautiful; it is a combination of two worlds, a world of vision and a world of matter. We need both worlds to find our way. We need the symbols of our vision and a concrete world in which to play out our visions.

Just the act of dreaming, the act of remembering your dreams, brings the male/female energies into balance within each person. The intuitive vision of dreaming needs to be played out in the concrete world of matter. The inner feminine vision needs to be expressed through masculine action in the world. The vision, the dream, is feminine energy. Men and women, by denying their dreamtime, by not remembering their dreams, deny their feminine side, and deny themselves balance.

Some people do not remember their dreams: They state flatly, "I don't dream." Their world is so concrete and so material that the visions of dreamtime cannot get past the walls of physical reality.

These people deny themselves a vast amount of knowledge. They are not in touch with their inner feminine visions.

A Map Of The Tracks

The following is a story from India, which I have paraphrased:

Imagine a train on a railroad track. In front of the train are many miles of tracks. The people on the train can see only what is immediately ahead and to either side of them but that does not mean the tracks ahead do not exist. The tracks still exist ten miles down the track, even though no one on the train can see them. The engineer of the train has a radio that keeps him in communication with what is ahead of him. Additionally, signposts are provided along the way that he has been trained to read. The people on the train generally have faith in the safety of the tracks ahead since they know that the engineer will use his radio communication to make certain that the tracks are clear.

At the time the train is on the track at mile two, for instance, many miles of tracks are ahead, ready to bring the train into its future. There are, of course, possibilities for change: possibilities for the train to use other side tracks, possibilities of adding and taking away cars, and possibilities of going in different directions, but only if the engineer of the train stays in communication with the person in charge of the tracks.

Our dreamtime is a map of the tracks ahead of us if we know how to interpret the symbols and if we stay in contact with that part of ourselves which is in charge of the tracks. By not being open to our dreams, we are denying ourselves the benefit of the map of the tracks.

Beginning Dreamwork

To understand your dreams it is important to begin a relationship with them. Having a relationship with a dream is no different than having a relationship with a person; one needs to invest energy and time in the relationship. Begin by simply recording your dreams and giving gratitude to your dream-maker. You will be swiftly rewarded by having more dreams. Even if you feel you do not understand the symbols, continue to record the dreams and see if there is any correlation between the dreams and your life.

Understanding your dreams is a process that does not occur overnight. However, once you start to unravel the symbols of your dreams, you will have begun a wonderful journey, a journey that will take you into both the ancient past and the unknown future, a journey that will give you hope and peace and a journey that you will begin to understand because you have guided it. You are the original mapmaker.

In *Dreams: Your Magic Mirror* by Elsie Sechrist, there are examples of what various symbols might mean. This book shares the wisdom of Edgar Cayce's dream analysis. I found that many times it did not have my symbols in it but, nevertheless, I was able to get clues from it about the possible meaning. Looking at my dreams with the help of the book about Edgar Cayce's work deepened my knowledge of dreamwork. I would like to pay special tribute to Elsie Sechrist for her influence on my dreamwork that laid the groundwork for some of this chapter.

Psychological Dreams

I divide dreams into three types: psychological, physical and spiritual. Psychological dreams consist of dreams that integrate our everyday activities. These dreams are essential for a healthy personality. Most of the time the meaning of these dreams is not particularly evident but I find they clear out the garbage of the day and prepare the mind for another day. I feel these dreams are the lowest level of dreaming. If you have had a bad day, some of the dreams that night will be merely to put the images into perspective in the mind, to integrate who you are with the outside world. Sometimes these dreams are deepening whatever learning you have accomplished during the day. It is easier to remember items for a test if you can sleep on it first. Even though you are sleeping, a part of the mind sorts out all the input it has received during the day and makes order out of chaos.

A deeper level dream but still in the category of psychological dreams, is the dream that attempts to heal the emotional part of the psychological structure of a person. These are the dreams that one usually takes into psychotherapy to heal the various hurts of being human on this planet. When I was in psychotherapy, most of the dreams I encountered were dreams that told me how I was hurt and how I could heal myself to interact more effectively in the world. This level of dreams looks at anger, fear, sadness, loneliness and the wounded child, and helps the individual connect each of those parts and go toward wholeness. These dreams look at our separateness from the world and from ourselves and help us to integrate the pieces of ourselves into a whole person.

Physical Dreams

The second type of dream concerns the physical body. For a human being to interact effectively in the world, the physical body needs to be healthy. In addition to a healthy psychological self, a healthy physical self is necessary, and, if at all possible, desirable. I find the dream-maker gives advice and warnings to those who can understand the symbols to keep the physical body in a healthy state.

Spiritual Dreams

The third type of dream is the spiritual dream, which is the highest level of dreaming. Spiritual dreams can originate from our own higher self, from the higher self of a loved one, or from the source of all of life, the universal God-energy. These dreams are always future oriented and contain great guidance for important life choices.

Example: Psychological Dream

The following is an example of a psychological dream I had soon after starting Gestalt therapy:

> I was standing at the entrance to a large, dark cave. There was a gossamer veil hanging at the entrance to the cave. Behind the veil on the left side of the opening, an old Indian woman was praying. I knew that I had to enter that cave and explore its darkness.

This was a beautiful dream which told me with very little symbolism that, although I had to look at the darkness within myself, I was protected by ancient powers within myself. I knew and felt that I would be safe in the darkness.

Gestalt therapy teaches that to understand your dream you must be each part of the dream. For instance, in my therapy session, my therapist would actually have me change chairs. Facing the chair I had been sitting in before helped to change my energy so that I would be able to become more connected to each image in the dream and therefore be more connected to myself.

In the foregoing dream, for instance, I was the gossamer veil, I was that part of myself which revealed the darkness. I was also the old Indian woman with ancient knowledge of how to navigate the darkness. I was praying over myself. I was also the darkness and the cave that held the darkness. Seeing the dream in this fashion helped me to own different aspects of myself and to go toward wholeness. My dream showed me with great clarity that I as the survivor had within me all the necessary ingredients for healing.

When working with a psychological dream in this way, it may take a few weeks to fully work the dream through to learn how to integrate it into your life. My dream showed that it was safe to look at the darkness but that it might take me some time to ready myself for that difficult task. The dream was my map, it showed me the way.

Example: Physical Health Dream

The following is an example of a physical health dream which I have had:

> I was standing in a bathroom. There were three bathtubs in front of me. They were very dirty, and I did not know how to clean them.

Three days after having the dream I was overcome with a terrible flu. I believe that if I had gone on a cleansing diet starting the morning I had the dream, I probably could have avoided the flu. At the time, though, I did not know what the symbols meant.

You will find that if you put in writing all of your dreams, you will begin to recognize a correlation between your dreams and your health. For instance, I can usually tell if a dream of mine is about my health because symbols of cleansing will be in the dream, such as a toilet, washing machine, bathroom sink, or dirty floor.

Example: Spiritual Dream

The most exciting dreams for me have been my spiritual dreams, my dreams that connect me to God, to my future. The following are some examples:

> A grey male wolf was staring at me. He was beautiful, magnif-icent. He was merely sitting. He was not frightening or menacing. There was nothing else to that dream, just the wolf staring at me.

The next night I had another dream.

> The wolf returned and brought his mate and two baby cubs. The she-wolf was lying on her side very relaxed and the cubs were playing. I picked up one of the fat, furry cubs, held it up to the sky and said, "I think I'll keep this one."

When I awoke, I became very excited because I knew it was a message of importance. However, at that time I was not able to understand anything about it. Two days later I was having a session with Melinda Miller and when I told her the dream, she became very excited and said, "You must be a member of the Wolf Clan Lodge!" I had no idea what she was talking about but I was curious. Unbeknown to me Melinda was a member of the Wolf Clan Teaching Lodge of the Seneca Nation. She told me to call Twylah Nitsch, head of the Lodge, and ask her if I could visit. My daughter and I then spent seven days at the lodge during the Harmonic Convergence in 1987. Twylah said a wolf always brings you there. Twylah has been very important in my healing process. I would never have met her if I had ignored the dream.

Another dream that had great meaning for me happened as follows:

> I wanted to cross a river. It was full of big boulders, and the water was deep, swift and wide. A man told me I would be able to cross it if I went back to the source. I walked along the side of the river for a long distance. In the dream it seemed to take forever but finally I came to a place where it was narrow and shallow.
>
> I crossed over and then found myself walking along a path. My daughter was on my left and a wonderfully strong, handsome man was on my right. We were walking with our arms intertwined behind our backs. I looked on the other side of the man and saw my chocolate Labrador retriever Cocoa. I was happy to see her and said, "Hi, Cocoa." The man was dressed in a red checkered flannel shirt and blue jeans. He reminded me of a lumberjack. In front of us was a beautiful mountain range.

I had this dream two years ago and have since found that it was truly a map of my future. Although I had worked very hard at healing the wounds of childhood sexual abuse, I had not previously gone back to the source, had not cleaned out the bottom of the garbage pail. Over the next two years I symbolically walked back to the source of this dangerous river, in order to get to the other side and to go on with my life with joy and happiness. I went back to the source of my pain in order to heal the cause of my wounds and to find a new path where I would be happy and be part of a family again.

The next two years brought the death of my father, the writing of this book and the continual releasing of layer after layer of pain. I moved into a new house, changed professions and entered graduate school. I feel I have crossed over the small stream and that I have integrated the child, the woman and the man within myself. The people on the path walking toward the mountain (which stands for transformation) are symbolic of the healed child, the healed woman and the strong gentle man being united within myself.

More Synchronicity

Another dream of mine that demonstrates a different aspect of a spiritual dream happened as follows:

> I was walking along a river and I was holding a telephone that was stretched around a boulder in front of me. I would not let go of the phone line and it put me off balance. I fell into the river. The strong current pulled me away from the bank and I was very frightened. However, when I was in the middle of the river, invisible hands held me up in the swift water. The hands took me upstream against the current and deposited me on the bank in an area of the river I had never previously seen. I laughed as I climbed out of the water and shook water out of my shoes.

This dream showed me how synchronicity can work in my life. Two days after having the dream I happened to see a program with Joseph Campbell on public television, *The Power of Myth,* in which he was saying that if you follow your bliss, you will feel like invisible hands are carrying you along.

Invisible hands were carrying me along in my dream. I was walking downstream but I was off balance from stretching myself too far. Falling into the river allowed me to get back on track and to participate in the universe supporting me and opening doors for me. The next few months were not easy months but they were full of new decisions, new doors opening and, in essence, a brand new life. The effect of the dream was one of reassurance that all of these new things were right and that I was on track.

Great Treasure

There is one last dream that I want to share with you. I had this dream a few months before I began to write this book:

> A man came to me and gave me a round rock the size of an orange. It was a plain brown rock. As I looked at it he said, "Let me show you!" He then poked at a place on the rock and loose sand fell out. Then he turned the rock upside down and all manner of

jewels fell out. Hunks of rose quartz, clear quartz crystals, rubies, emeralds and diamonds came pouring out. The treasure from inside the small rock actually made a pile on the ground the size of a small mountain, many times bigger than the rock. I just stood there staring at the treasure.

The man in the dream has come to me often in dreams. When he comes, he always bears a gift of great significance. I assume he is one of my guides because whatever he does in the dream concerns my spiritual growth.

His gift seemed plain at first, of no value. Then there appeared a hole in the solid-looking rock which was plugged only with sand. It took only a small touch to unplug it. The miracle then happened: A rock the size of an orange poured treasure a hundred times its size, all of immeasurable value. (Rose quartz crystal heals the heart, clear quartz brings clarity, emerald heals father issues, ruby heals mother issues and diamond heals one's spiritual self.)

As the year went on I realized that the rock was me and the treasure was this book, which not only healed me as I wrote it but which I believe can also help heal other men and women of the wounds in their lives.

Dreams are indeed the windows to the self and if we are willing to undertake the work, they will provide enormous help to us on our journey of healing childhood sexual abuse.

11

Healing Physical And Spiritual Boundaries

Dream

It was nighttime. I was looking up at the sky. In the sky was a beautiful Indian shield. It was very large. Inside the shield was a beautiful brown horse. Next to the horse was a beautiful young girl with flowing hair similar to the horse's mane. The girl was very happy. Feathers were hanging off the shield at the one o'clock and seven o'clock positions on the circle.

After I was raped and molested at five, I was different. I was different in a way that until recent years I could not put into words. That difference has affected every relationship of mine since then.

After the abuse in my own bedroom, I have never again been the same — more than the pain, more than the humiliation, more than the fear, more than the anger, more than all of these put together — something else was wrong.

As a child I tried to understand it. I carefully watched other people trying to understand why I was different. I would set up cues to live my life by but I could never believe that I was like anyone else. I would watch how other people told jokes and I would try to tell them the same way but it never felt as though it worked for me. When I told a joke, it was invariably at the wrong time or to the wrong people.

I was clumsy socially. I would bump into people both literally and figuratively. I was inappropriate when speaking to someone else. I would try very hard to say the right thing but somehow it always felt as though it came out the wrong way. Sometimes, even when I felt I said the right thing, I would misinterpret the reaction of others and then say something very awkward.

Still, I searched for clues. I so wanted to be like everyone else. I could not understand why I felt different. When I looked in the mirror, I did not see any difference but when I interacted with other people, a different reaction seemed to occur. Tension developed when no one else had tension. I felt alone and isolated. This feeling of loneliness and isolation had been a part of my life for as long as I could remember.

Physical And Spiritual Boundaries

Over the last few years of healing I have come to realize the nature of my feeling of difference. It has nothing to do with anger, fear, depression or embarrassment. It has to do with boundaries. My physical, psychological and spiritual boundaries were damaged. The damage to my boundaries has been the cause of my feeling of being so different.

Principally, in this chapter, I am referring to the physical boundaries, and energy or spiritual boundaries, and not the psychological boundaries, although there is some overlap. Marsha Utain, in the book *Scream Louder* which she co-authored with Barbara Oliver, has an excellent discussion on psychological boundaries and I strongly recommend it. However, my intention here is to introduce you to some ideas concerning the healing of the boundaries on the physical and energy levels.

Energy Boundaries

When a child is born, there is a beautiful natural boundary of energy all around that child. This boundary of energy is full of vibrant colors, although not everyone easily sees them. I believe that when we look at babies, we come the closest to seeing auras, even for those people who have difficulty believing in auras.

We are all composed of energy. This energy not only surrounds us, it also culminates in centers along the spine, called chakras. Chakras form the basis of our energy boundaries.

Imagine a person in front of you. Surrounding this person for about a foot in each direction is an invisible boundary of energy. Make it visible in your mind by ascribing colors to it: greens, yellows, blues, violets. These colors do not just sit still, they are constantly moving as all energy does. This person has intact boundaries, her boundaries have never been invaded.

The energy surrounding the body of a person who has been sexually abused as a child is very different. The vibrant colors can be missing or are not as strong. In their place are shields of armor. The shields vary in thickness and content. Some shields are made of hate, some are made of fear and some are made of fat. The colors of these shields are often dark, muddy and heavy.

Healing Boundaries

Melinda Miller has taught me a method of healing the shields or holes in the energy boundaries. Quietly go into a meditative space and when your energy is centered, visualize a clear plastic mannequin standing in front of you. This statue symbolizes your energy boundaries. As you see the mannequin look for any cracks, holes or thick areas in it. When I first started using this visualization, my entire pelvic area was missing.

In your visualization make a mixture of healing paste. You can put anything you want into it: flowers, mother-of-pearl, pine trees, pink quartz crystal. When your mixture is just right, apply it lovingly to the damaged areas in the mannequin. Take loving care as you visualize the healing of your energy boundaries. Spend as much time as you need for the healing. Repeat this visualization until you can see clearly that your energy boundaries have been and now remain healed.

Sensory System Shut-Down

In addition to the damage to the energy boundaries, a response that every child can also experience as a result of rape is a shut-down of her sensory system. This shut-down acts as a protective mechanism in order to help minimize the child's pain. If the child feels less pain, the child can more readily go on with her life. There is a high price to pay, however, for feeling less pain.

The sensory system is the part of the nervous system that receives touch and then interprets it, translating to the person what the nature of the sensation is — warmth, cold, pleasant touch, unpleasant touch. This touch system is part of the physical boundary system and it greatly contributes to our sense of boundaries as human beings.

As a physical therapist I have worked with many children who have had damage to their touch systems, resulting in their brains misinterpreting the sensation of touch that occurred at their skin level. A pleasant touch was often interpreted by the child as unpleasant. When the child's mother touched the child lovingly, the child would frequently pull away because her touch system would interpret it as unpleasant.

For a child who has been raped, the damage to the touch system is not in the brain. The damage to the child who has been raped is external: It is on the skin, in the vagina and genital area, all over the body. The pain was so great to the child that the psyche of the child told the brain to shut down. The child did not want to experience the pain and the brain accommodated it, shutting down a portion of the touch system. The child's subconscious mind regulated the part of the brain that interpreted touch.

This shut-down of the touch system has many ramifications for the child and for the adult she later becomes. It has the same effect on the child who is raped as the child who has damage to her central touch system. Both children misinterpret touch. Both children will pull away from loving touch because their brains interpret it as painful, uncomfortable.

This disruption of the touch boundaries is based on the belief system "Touch hurts and I cannot be touched." These are strong thought forms that the subconscious mind has created out of the rape. These thought forms need to be changed if we are to enjoy being touched again.

Inventory Safe Types Of Touching

To begin healing the damaged touch system, make a list of where on your body you feel it is safe to be touched and also what kind of touch feels good. For example:

- A mild spray from a shower anywhere on my body feels good.
- Soft cotton clothes worn from head to toe comfort me.
- My dog and cat can touch me on my body.
- Riding horseback gives me pleasurable touch.
- My best friend can hold my hand.
- My lover can touch my feet and my legs below my knees.

By making this list as long as possible you are beginning to diminish the impact of the belief system that you cannot be touched without it hurting. Exhaust the possibilities in making the list. Then if the areas that can be touched without pain and fear change, add those changes to the list. Belief systems can be changed and damaged boundaries can be healed.

Rhythm And Boundaries

A person feels out of sync with the rest of the world and no longer in rhythm with people when her boundaries have been damaged. When a child as young as five has been raped, that child thereafter does not know where she ends and another person begins. If a child of five is out of sync, the normal bonding of that child with parents, siblings and friends becomes disrupted and disconnected. That child then misses out on a considerable amount of learning through normal social interactions.

With the child's normal boundary of touch drastically altered, the child now needs to fabricate new boundaries. However, these new boundaries are now built for protection, not for rhythm and synchrony. When new boundaries are clumsily built for protection, they have unusual gaps and holes.

Trust

The sad paradox about a child who has been raped is that she, on the one hand, does not trust trustworthy people and relationships but, on the other hand, she places her blind faith in people who are not trustworthy. The child's ability to make worthy judgments about people has been damaged. A woman I knew who as a child was repeatedly raped by her father constantly exposed her body inappropriately to people without even realizing she was doing it, while at the same time maintaining a wide boundary of anger and fear around her. On the one hand, she appeared to permit people to get too close to her. On the other hand, however, no one was able to be close to her at all.

People who have been sexually abused as children frequently find that becoming overweight is a solution to missing and damaged boundaries. The fat fills in that space around the person which previously was filled with beautiful colors. The fat becomes an armor of sorts. When I am overweight, I feel more protected. There is a heaviness that makes me feel more solid.

I can be very successful with a diet until something in my world makes me afraid. Then I eat until at least a few pounds have returned and I feel safe again. It is that lightness of being, both spiritually and physically, that is uncomfortable.

The Healing Touch Of Massage

One way that has helped me to heal my physical boundaries has been through massage. During a period of seven years I have been to a number of therapists for the healing touch of massage. Often, when I was receiving a massage the pain stored in my physical body would be released and I would cry and would have the need to talk about a memory. It was important that these therapists knew about abuse and how to listen to me.

When the body therapist combines knowledge of the physical body with knowledge of the energy systems, healing occurs simultaneously on both levels. Sometimes I find a visualization can also be combined with the massage or that I can silently repeat an affirmation to myself. For me, this helps to heal my body, mind and energy systems.

I have found it very difficult to heal my damaged boundaries. I believe that to successfully do so takes great perseverance with considerable openness to new ideas. Since part of the damage originally was to my energy system, I have found that some of the solutions which have been helpful to me require working with energy.

Energy Imagery

My friend and teacher Melinda Miller has worked with the healing energies for years, and her *Rainbow Dancer* contains many exercises to heal ourselves through energy.

A wonderful boundary of energy that Melinda teaches is the "blue sword of protection." In any situation where you feel uncomfortable or vulnerable, visualize an imaginary indigo blue sword in front of you, in back of you, to the right of you, to the left of you, above you and below you. These swords of light will protect you on an energy level. Do you remember the sword of light that Luke Skywalker used in *Star Wars?* These shields of indigo blue energy you now have surrounding you have the same power of protection.

When people question why I believe that visualizing light can be powerful, I remind them of how powerful light is in our world. Laser beams can cut through tissue and solid objects, yet, in truth, the beams are only light. Try experimenting with this new way of healing your wounds. You will find yourself becoming lighter and lighter as your heaviness is discarded.

For another experience with energy, Melinda recommends visualizing yourself standing in a crystal pyramid. Take a moment and make it as detailed as possible. Crystals are exquisitely beautiful and in your mind's eye you are able to stand in one. Visualize a fountain of clear water flowing upward through you from deep within the earth. Stay in the cleansing pyramid as long as you desire. Melinda teaches that these fountains of crystal clear waters refresh you and help you to experience wholeness.

After each of these experiences with energy, take a moment to give thanks. Gratitude connects you with everything in the universe and completes the cycle of healing.

American Indian Animal Power

The Native American culture also has ways to heal boundaries. I recently read *Medicine Cards* by Jamie Sams and David Carson. It is an excellent book on the discovery of power through the ways of animals. Jamie and David talk about the boundaries that an armadillo can teach. I was very excited when they suggested making a medicine shield. I had worked with medicine shields with Melinda Miller but it had never occurred to me that it was teaching me boundaries.

To fully understand the use of animal power you will need to read *Medicine Cards*. I would like to share with you my experience with using the armadillo medicine shield. As Jamie and David suggest, I drew a circle on a sheet of paper. Inside the circle I put anything that I wanted to "have, do or to experience." On the outside of the shield, as they suggest, I put what I was "willing to experience by invitation only." For me, I began to experience a clearer boundary around myself, as well as to get better in touch with what I really wanted. As they indicated in the book I became clearer both to myself and to others.

Armadillo medicine is very healing for survivors of sexual abuse. I recommend using it at least once a week. Make a new shield each week because, as you experiment with boundaries, what you put in the middle of the shield will change. Also, what you are willing to put on the outside of your shield will change as your boundaries improve. Tack the medicine shields on your wall or on your refrigerator to remind you that you now have boundaries that you have made yourself, new boundaries that are not made of hate and anger and fat.

Rainbow Shields Of Power

Using the basic instructions that Jamie and David suggest, I have tried different ways to use the shield. One which I have enjoyed is drawing an outline of my inner child in the middle of the shield. Then, using colored pencils, I draw in boundaries of energy in any way that feels right to me at the time. I am careful to leave no area blank. I pay special loving attention to the area around my pelvis and vagina, using only the colors of the rainbow. We have all had enough darkness in our lives.

For another variation, take a very large sheet of paper and draw your protective shield as large as you can. Inside the shield, draw an outline of yourself that fills the complete circle. Next, draw your inner child inside you. Do all the drawing with loving care because you are drawing the new you. The new you has a protective shield and a healed inner child. Next, add the colors of the rainbow to you and your inner child. Isn't it beautiful to see yourself glow? You cannot do this exercise too many times.

Put the pictures all over your room and feel the pleasure of your healed boundaries. I call these shields my rainbow shields of power. I would like to pay special tribute to Jamie Sams and David Carson for sharing their knowledge with the world for it has made a difference in my life.

Medicine Wheel Of Peace

Each year I honor the healing energies of the changing of the seasons by walking the Medicine Wheel of Peace at the spring and fall equinoxes and the summer and winter solstices. After reading *Medicine Cards* I have now added making an armadillo medicine shield to my ceremony at the winter solstice. My daughter and I both do it and I have found that it is very powerful.

Melinda Miller has also taught me that the winter solstice is the time of the year when it is important to plant the seeds that we want to grow over the next year. In *Rainbow Dancer,* Melinda and Jane share that "the winter solstice, in late December, begins an important cycle in life. In the winter, the earth lies dormant, at rest. We take the opportunity to ask ourselves, 'What do I want? Where am I going?, What seed shall I plant for my life? The tiny seeds nestle in our hearts until the spring equinox, in late March."

When I was ready to plant my seeds, I drew the shield. Inside the circle I wrote all the things that I wanted to accomplish for the next year, the seeds of new beginnings. Then when I walked the medicine wheel with several other people, I firmed up the boundaries of my armadillo medicine by keeping the shield in my mind as I said prayers of gratitude to the Great Spirit.

I would try to look at the shield at different intervals. At the spring equinox I would again reaffirm the energy of the shield and give new prayers to these seedlings that need tending over the next few months.

The fall equinox is a time of harvesting and of giving thanks. The seeds we sow in December are grown to fruition during the warm summer months and are now ready to be harvested. Look back again at your medicine shield and make certain that you remember to harvest all that you have planted so that you can come to completion and experience satisfaction.

Experiencing completion and satisfaction are difficult for survivors. By walking the Medicine Wheel of Peace each year we can allow ourselves the pleasure of harvesting our own accomplishments. It will give us a sense of empowerment.

Experiment with armadillo medicine and make some medicine shields to build new boundaries. You will be surprised at the results in your life.

Fear And The Space It Leaves

It is important to remember why we have boundaries of armor around us in the first place. I believe that healing our boundaries brings up a great deal of fear in us. The fear and the terror of a child who has been sexually abused is enormous. I had forgotten about the terror until recently when I had a dream which reminded me of this all-encompassing emotion. When a child experiences terror, the child knows her life is at stake. As you change your boundaries these feelings of fear will surface and can be very unpleasant.

As you are working with the formation of new boundaries and the fear surfaces, simply release it. You may want to explore it with your therapist or you may want to use a releasing technique I will share with you later but something Melinda has shared with me is important to remember: Thoughts and feelings take up space and when you talk about the fear and look at it, it leaves a space. This space then needs to be filled with light or love or joy or it will be filled with the first negative emotion that comes along.

This was a difficult concept for me to understand until I began to think back to when I was in therapy. I would be in a therapy session and would be looking at sadness or fear or anger. Immediately after the session I would feel better. In a few hours, however, I found that I would be experiencing negative emotions again. It was not until I began working with energy that I was able to release emotions and make room for joy. I realized I had room for joy because I was filling the empty space with joy.

You also can fill the space with color once you begin to become familiar with the energies of each color. Try doing so the next time you are dealing with negative emotions. Release your negative emotions in any way you know how. Visualize, in your mind, filling the space with whatever you feel you need at the moment. You are your own best judge of what you need: unconditional love, joy, peace, giggles, lightness.

"The Let Go"

An excellent technique that Melinda has taught me to use to release negative feelings of any kind is called "The Let Go." Place one hand on your forehead and the other hand on your navel: Feel all your worries, fears, anger or other emotions lifting from you into the big blue sky. Then feel warm, gentle winds blowing through you from the deep green forest. Give gratitude to the blue sky and the deep green forest.

This exercise incorporates a release of negative energy and a filling up with positive energy. Try this during your day to release the small bothersome parts of your life. You will have a pleasant surprise. You will not only feel better but you also will find that you are continuing to feel better.

We have been hurt by people and healing with the energies of Mother Earth is one of the safest places you can be. We have never been hurt by an armadillo or a crystal pyramid. There are no negative images in our minds concerning these new healing images. Working with these archetypal images also will circumvent the conscious mind because the unconscious mind recognizes these ancient archetypal images and begins to heal without conscious thought.

Walk with your new boundaries of color, talk with your new boundaries of color, hear with your new boundaries of color and you will begin to see your true beauty again.

12

An Encounter With Healing Sounds

"In the beginning was the Word, and the Word was with God, and the Word was God."

John 1:1

"In the beginning was the Word (Sound) . . ."

Sound Medicine
by Leah Maggie Garfield

The following is a story of my own personal encounter with the healing energies of sound.

One Sunday I was spending a quiet day alone at home. For no apparent reason the thought suddenly occurred to me to go to South Street and browse through book stores. This was a period of time when I was reading a great deal and I decided to follow my inner guide. One of my favorite stores is Garland of Letters. The woman who operates this bookstore always permits browsing to your heart's content. After what felt like a long time I finally noticed an author whom I recognized, Leah Maggie Garfield. The book of hers which I knew well was titled *Companions in Spirit.* I became excited because I now noticed another book by her, one entitled *Sound Medicine.* I had been trying at the time to heal a herniated disk in my lower back, as well as continuing to heal my wounded child, and I was captivated with the title and the author. I, of course, bought the book.

The Healing Song

Sunday nights are usually busy at my house because my daughter normally returns after a visit with her father. I did not get an opportunity to truly look at the book until bedtime. I found myself drawn to the chapter on the healing song. To fully understand the healing song you will need to read the book. I would like, however, to share with you my journey into sound.

As I read the chapter I found myself becoming more and more excited. As described by the author, the healing song felt to me like a wonderful companion to have with me on the journey of healing my inner wounded child. I felt frustrated, though, because it seemed very complicated to find my own healing song and I did not think I knew anyone who could help me. As I fell asleep that night I realized that finding my own healing song was very much on my mind. In the middle of the night I was awakened by the following dream:

> I was with a group of people who were looking for their healing songs. We went outside and formed a circle. The man next to me in the circle received his healing song immediately and he then sang it to me. We laughed and cried when we heard the beauty of the song. I worked and worked but could not find mine. I awoke from the dream without my song.

As soon as I awakened I knew that the song the man in my dream found was actually mine. I sang it to myself for a while and then went back to sleep. I knew I would not forget it because it was very similar to the song in *Close Encounters of the Third Kind.*

When I awakened the next morning I immediately wrote the song in my journal. I sang my new song to myself at every free moment that day.

A Deep Contentment

The feelings the song generated inside of me were indescribable. The sounds made me feel content inside, a deep contentment I had never previously experienced, other than being loved by someone else. However, this time the contentment was coming from deep inside myself. A person who has been sexually abused as a child loses the ability to make herself feel better; she loses that internal contentment that helps her feel good about herself. I found my healing song to be one more avenue toward self-respect, one more road toward wholeness.

In *Sound Medicine,* the author said to let the song change if it wanted to. My song changed quite a bit over the next few days and then it did not change anymore. I felt the energy of my song strongest and most healing in the area of my emotional heart. For the next few days I sang my song anytime I was alone.

The Life Song

Leah Maggie Garfield speaks firmly about the rules concerning the healing song and I have respected them. A few days later I picked up the book again and read the next few pages. She described another song of power—the life song. I again found myself becoming very excited but, also again, I followed her directions. She instructed that one should not look for the life song for several days after finding the healing song.

Several days later I was lying in bed and Paul Simon's album *Graceland* came to mind. I was almost asleep but at the same time I was enjoying the twilight before sleep takes over. I thought of the African sounds of his album and about how much those sounds feel familiar to me. I then became aware of a tune in my head. It had sounds, it had notes and it was very simple.

Immediately I became wide awake. My life song . . . it was my life song. I grabbed my journal because this time I knew I would not remember it. I wrote it in my journal and then I fell asleep. The next morning I looked in my journal and then sang my life song. It did not have much of an impact on me then. I decided to leave it alone for a while and just enjoyed the contentment of my healing song. That was November 9th.

At the beginning of December I decided to buy my daughter a synthesizer for Christmas but I felt that I could not wait until Christmas. I thought of an excuse to give it to her early. I confess I was really giving it to me. I was driven to try my songs on the instrument. First, I played my healing song on it. My healing song sounded comforting on the synthesizer but I was taken entirely by surprise when I played my life song. Every cell in my body vibrated to the sounds of my life song! I played it again. It happened again! My God, I had never experienced anything like this before. I continued to play. The song changed a little but then stabilized and has remained the same since then. I have now sung this song many times and it has never failed to have a strong impact on my entire body.

Resonance . . . it feels like my cells vibrate to the notes and sounds and that it awakens the core of who I am. Garfield states that one gets the life song right before a major change occurs in that person's life. That has certainly been my situation. I know that both my healing song and my life song will always be with me.

Our Souls' Sounds

It is very possible that *in the beginning was Sound, and the Sound was with God, and the Sound was God.* I believe our souls are built on the sounds of those original notes and that those sounds come into our lives again to remind us of our life's purpose. Steven Spielberg had part of a universal truth when he used that particular song in his movie *Close Encounters of the Third Kind.* The song in the movie reminded us of our source, our creator and it rang true in each and every one of us. Those notes and sounds have resonance in every cell of our bodies.

"Resonant" is defined in the *Merriam-Webster Dictionary* as "continuing to sound." The sounds that my soul have been imprinted upon are continuing to sound, are continuing to be resonant. Perhaps death has to do with the resonance changing as we transform our energy into another form.

Recently the life song began singing itself inside of me again. It came at a period of time when I was discouraged while editing this book. The song seems to sing itself. I do not choose when it sings inside of me. It may be that the singing of my life song is heralding more than the completion of this book. Part of the beauty of the song is its mystery.

13

Courage:
The Lion Within

Take Care of Me Visualization Exercise: Place your left hand over the navel and the other hand on your back directly opposite the left hand. Imagine riding on a chestnut horse into the orange sunset. Be grateful for strong chestnut horses and sunsets.

Rainbow Dancer
by Melinda Miller
and Jane Rachfalski

The lion within is courage. The *Merriam-Webster Dictionary* defines courage as the ability to conquer fear. I would rather use the word transform instead of conquer. Courage is the ability to transform fear into something else. Courage transforms fear into survival, courage transforms fear into power and courage transforms fear into love.

Courage is transformational—it is able to change one form of energy into another form of energy. Courage is not love and it is not fear. It is that vital ingredient—that wonderful energy—that is necessary for survival of the person sexually abused as a child. It is the bricks and mortar of the foundation of survival and like the Cowardly Lion in the *Wizard of Oz* who has had it all along, so have we.

There is more than one type of courage. Courage is like a single quartz crystal mined from the earth. Each facet of the quartz crystal is unique and slightly different from every other facet. Each facet of courage is different but like the crystal, the strength and beauty of courage comes from its unity, its oneness and its clarity as it is seen and perceived.

Courage of Survival

There is the basic courage of survival. The energy for this courage comes from the creative energy of the genital area — that sacred area where our life force is generated. This is the courage I had when my father was pushing the pillow into my face and suffocating me. I had the courage to give up fighting in order to live. I survived at any cost. In truth, I am glad that my life force was so strong, that I had the courage to live. I actually saved my life but the price I had to pay was enormous.

The pattern of giving up instead of fighting was ingrained in my subconscious mind for many years. The hypnotist I saw several years ago explained to me that the subconscious mind interpreted what happened to me as follows: In order to live I had to give up, therefore, in my subconscious mind, if I fight I will die. It has been hard all of my life to fight for what I really want, to go all out for me. My pattern has been to let the other person win, especially if the other person was male. This pattern has mostly left my life now but it was a gradual healing that took considerable practice.

Courage Of Strength

Another facet of courage is the internal strength to take power in the world. An example of this strength is the courage to go into psychotherapy and to begin the process of healing the wounded child within. It is a very rigorous process but very necessary in order to reclaim your life and enter another level of courage. To go back and look at what happened and to heal the wounds takes enormous courage. But the pain does go away and it is possible to make a happy rewarding life for yourself.

For me pain was a teacher. I was in so much emotional pain, I kept searching for more answers — sometimes undefinable, sometimes illusive, sometimes maddeningly hard to get to. I was always able to dig deep enough into that bottomless well and never completely give up. My search brought me healing because I had courage.

Courage Of The Heart

Van Morrison, in his song *Listen to the Lion,* captured the essence of the transformational quality of courage. The courage that Van Morrison so beautifully sings about is the courage originating from the energy center of the emotional heart. When I chose to survive as my father was suffocating me, that courage came from the basic courage of survival. When I chose to love myself, when I chose to love the wounded child within me, that courage came from the heart.

The courage of the heart is qualitatively different because the energy of the heart is different from the energy of the genital area which is where the survival courage originates. The energy of the heart has more power to transform fear, more creative power to make changes in your life and more healing power for the wounded child within. As people learn to develop the heart energy, they will find a limitless amount of energy available to them, and the energy will be of the highest quality.

Getting Back To Kansas

I recently saw *The Wizard of Oz* again. I watched it with new eyes, so to speak. I saw Dorothy's journey as a journey within to deal with the fear in her life. She was in a stage of transition and she had to look at her fear. As usual, the fear was covered up by anger, which can be a more useful emotion, and the tornado of her anger took her on her journey; it furnished the energy to go within to search for the three things that she needed in her life — the ability to think, the strength of courage, and the energy of the heart. All of us have within us from time to time, straw instead of brains, an armor of tin around our hearts and a blustery fake courage; the Scarecrow, the Tin Man and the Cowardly Lion are not foreign to any of us.

Dorothy's inward journey was not unlike the journey that occurs in psychotherapy. A survivor of incest decides to seek help from a therapist usually when she is in a stage of transition; the survivor does not want to live with the pain anymore but at the same time does not know where she is going, where the therapy will take her. The survivor then takes the yellow brick road. The yellow brick road of therapy is no different than the yellow brick road that Dorothy decided to follow.

For Dorothy to get back to Kansas she had to pass through many obstacles, many tests of her thinking abilities, of the development of her heart and of her courage. Getting back to Kansas for Dorothy signified that she integrated the things she had been seeking, that she integrated thinking, heart and courage into herself and made herself whole. The survivor of incest also has to get back to Kansas. The survivor of incest has things to integrate on her yellow brick road. The survivor also has to find and integrate her thinking, her heart and her courage.

For Dorothy, the yellow brick road was not always pleasant; it was filled with pitfalls, danger and considerable fear. So also with psychotherapy, the survivor has a difficult journey in front of her but, as with Dorothy, there is help along the way. When Dorothy was really stuck, Glynda, the Good Witch of the North, was there to help. We all have our good witches who are there in time of need. Sometimes it is an internal strength that is suddenly available. Sometimes it is a friend who loves you and sees your beauty and helps you over a hard place. Sometimes it is the life force energy of the universe that people call God. This God/Goddess energy is always available, we only have to ask.

14

Forgiveness

Dream

I was walking up a steep mountain with a young girl. She fell a little behind and I walked back and picked her up. As we rounded the last bend together we arrived on the top of the mountain. We were awestruck at what we saw. In front of us an entire panoramic view of snow-capped mountains and waterfalls came into sight. We sat down with our arms around each other and tears rolled down our faces as we quietly looked at the beauty before us.

Many years ago I backpacked into the Sierra Nevada Mountains in California and while walking through some of the most beautiful country on this earth, I learned a valuable lesson that has stayed with me over the years.

I was traveling with several friends. We would awaken in the morning to the smell of the pines mixed with the dew that had dropped on the earth during the night. We would splash ice cold water on our faces, stumble over to the dead camp fire and build a small fire to heat water for the oatmeal and hot drinks. On this particular morning we packed our packs carefully. We knew we had a hard climb ahead of us to get over one of the difficult passes in the Sierra Madre range of mountains.

This was the most difficult part of the trek into the wilderness for me. Some passes were worse than others, but every pass had its breaking point for me where the climb seemed endless. The sensation of not getting anywhere surrounded every ache and pain.

My hiking companions were more experienced than I was and were always ahead of me on these upward climbs. About midday the coolness of the mountain morning was gone and in its place was a stale heat with no breeze in sight. My shoulder straps were digging deep into my shoulders. I was having trouble breathing in the high altitude. I would look to the horizon trying to spot the pass and trying to get some semblance of hope that this pain would soon end. I took several breaks. I kept wishing I was on top of the pass but no matter how much I wished myself at the end of my journey with my pack on the ground next to me, I was still sitting on the trail several hours away from the top of the pass.

The Inner Journey

The lesson I learned while my muscles ached on my journey up the mountain to the point of illumination, was that on our journey up the mountain of our lives, we can only be where we are at that very moment. We can wish and hope all we want but if the mountain pass is three miles straight up, then we still have three difficult miles of hiking ahead of us.

I also learned that you are at risk of losing your life if you sit down next to the trail and stay there too long. Being halfway to your goal is still being halfway to your goal. If you have carried provisions for six days, one extra day in the wilderness could be disastrous.

In my journey to heal my wounded child I have wished myself at the end of my journey many times because the miles ahead of me have seemed endless and I was already in so much pain. No amount of wishing changed the situation around me. I have had to take one careful step after another, constantly learning how to navigate the part of the mountain I was on at that moment, having some vague sense of the beauty at the top of the pass while at the same time dealing with sudden storms, millions of mosquitoes and the crossing of swollen rivers.

The pinnacle of my healing journey has been the *beginning* of understanding of what forgiveness is — both of my inner wounded child and of my parents. Several years ago when people strongly suggested I had to forgive my parents, I was not even close to understanding what that meant. The good intentions, unfortunately, only created more guilt and confusion rather than healing. If on the journey up the mountain of healing you find you cannot think about forgiveness, then at least give gratitude to yourself for being so perceptive and continue your walk up the mountain, tackling only what you are capable of handling and what is directly in front of you.

Cocoon Of Transformation

When my mother was a third-grade schoolteacher she brought caterpillars to school to give the children a lesson in metamorphosis. The children were all very excited and watched entranced as the caterpillars spun themselves into their self-made darkness, their cocoon of transformation. When the first cocoon hatched, the process took a full day, a full 24 hours. The emerging butterfly struggled and struggled through a tiny hole in the cocoon and finally became a beautiful butterfly, flying away.

The children were awestruck that the ugly worm could become a beautiful butterfly, but they were also impatient. One child in particular wanted to shorten the process. He did not see why it should take a full day. He saw that the only problem was the hole

was too small. With my mother's permission, he carefully enlarged
the hole of the next emerging butterfly. In only four hours the
butterfly emerged but its wings were undeveloped and weak and
the butterfly could not fly. It soon died, unable to fly off and lay eggs
and continue the cycle of transformation.

For total transformation of caterpillar to butterfly the struggle
within the darkness of the cocoon was necessary. For the development of the wings, for the butterfly to take flight, the wings had to
push and pull and strive with its entire being and when the boy
wanted to make it easier, he crippled the butterfly. The butterfly was
denied the growth of the struggle to live and to be transformed.

Healing Struggle

In our transformation of wounded child to loving adult, we also
have a metamorphosis to experience and if we are to fly, we have to
struggle within the darkness of our own cocoon. We are our own
guide, just as the butterfly is its own guide, and we each have our
own timing. Although I was always the last one to reach the pass, it
is important not to forget that I did reach it. If I had tried to hike at
the pace of the others, I could have jeopardized my journey with an
accident or sickness.

The timing of your healing is a very personal matter. You can only
take on what you are prepared for. When the survivor of childhood
sexual abuse realizes what her own timing is, an important change
will begin to occur in her healing process. A power will begin to
grow within her. The person is no longer a victim of the rape. She
is now in control of her own healing process. Therapists or friends
shall begin to take a back seat and the emerging person, the complex beautiful butterfly emerging from the cocoon of darkness, will
be in control of her own transformation.

What Forgiveness Isn't

I would like to share with you what I believe forgiveness is not.
Forgiveness is not letting people walk all over you. As survivors of
childhood sexual abuse, we very often find it difficult to speak up
when wronged. Sometimes we think we are getting along well with
people precisely because we do not want to rock the boat and we
are afraid of someone getting angry with us.

My mother thought she was being a good Christian when she
turned the other cheek and lived a very passive life. She lived her life
so passively that she permitted her husband to kill my cats and to

rape me. She always taught me to forgive, no matter what people did to me. The truth is my mother had little self-worth. She never felt herself worthy enough to say, "You cannot do this to me nor can you do this to my daughter." The combination of my mother's teachings of "turning the other cheek" and the powerlessness inherent in the rapes themselves created havoc with my ability to have happy relationships with others.

One way that women with little self-worth manage in the world is to learn to manipulate behind the scenes. Isn't it interesting that one of the things people hate worst about women is their manipulation? Isn't it also interesting that the reason we are manipulative is because we have been so oppressed for so many centuries? People who have been oppressed have little self-worth. They learn compensatory ways to get what they want.

Forgiving people for not treating us well is not helping us have self-worth. For true forgiveness to be possible in a person who has been sexually abused as a child, first that person has to develop self-worth and to stop letting people push her around. First that person has to consider herself important enough to say, "No more!" No more will I be treated like a door mat, no more will I be treated like a second class citizen and no more will I be ignored. "You have done me wrong and I will not have it any longer," needs to be said over and over until people start looking at you differently and until you see yourself differently.

Denial

The following story is a compilation of several stories that have been shared with me. I have chosen to call the fictitious survivor Sarah. It goes as follows:

"You know, my father was always after me," Sarah told me in a matter-of-fact tone.

I looked at her, trying not to show my surprise, and said. "What do you mean, 'always after you?'"

She again stated in a flat voice, "Well, at one time we thought I was pregnant."

"So, he didn't just bother you, he actually raped you?"

"I don't call it rape."

I told myself to be careful but I wanted to know more about an incident that wasn't rape but where pregnancy was feared. I asked quietly, "Did he penetrate you?"

"Yes."

"Did you want it to happen? Did you ask him to do this?"

She answered, "No, no, I didn't want it to happen."

"Your father had intercourse with you without your permission and you don't call it rape?" I asked incredulously.

Her demeanor was calm on the surface, as if she were talking about her favorite recipe. "No," she answered, "I've let it go. I don't hold it against him. He would thank me for this, if anyone asked him. He would thank me for the way I've handled this. He's a really nice man."

I didn't ask her why she needed him to thank her for her handling of the rape. I already knew the answer and I knew she was not ready to look at that issue. I also avoided the "nice man" comment for the moment. I then asked, "Did you go into therapy with anyone? Have you been able to talk to anyone about what happened?"

She responded quickly, "Oh no, I didn't need therapy, I was able to talk it out with my friends and I have completely let it go."

I then asked, "Is your mother still married to him?"

"Oh yes, they're very happily married. He's really a nice man."

I wanted to know more, and she didn't seem to mind talking with me. I asked her to tell me more about the incident.

"I was 10 when it started and it lasted for a while, and finally I made him stop. He didn't like that but he stopped. He did things to me after that which let me know he was mad at me. When I needed money for a car so I could get a job, he wouldn't help me. That was okay — I just figured out another way to do it. It made me stronger to do it by myself. I have really let it all go. That's the way I've handled it. I'm really just fine and they're happily married. He's really a nice man."

I knew I couldn't ask any more questions and that this women was sitting on a keg of dynamite. I also knew it would be very destructive if the wrong thing was said to her but I felt that I had to say something.

I finally decided to say, "I want to share with you just one thought, Sarah — that I admire you very much for what you have accomplished in your life. With all this pain you have a high position in your company and you seem to be doing well in your life. There's just one thing I want you to keep in mind — that somewhere inside you is a wounded child. Somewhere inside you is a 10-year-old girl who is hurting. It might not be tomorrow or it might not be in five years but someday in this lifetime you will need to acknowledge that wounded child and heal her to be really happy."

As she looked back at me, a wave of sadness swept over her face and I saw a 10-year-old girl in front of me. She was short and boyish with long, straight, blond hair. She wore clothes that hid her beauty and there was a prepubescent look about her. She had already shared with me that she had never been a sexually active person since the episodes with her father. As we said goodbye I gave her a big hug.

Taking On The Sins Of The Father

This woman felt she had forgiven her father, that she had released the incident from her life. What Sarah had done concerning the incident with her father was, in fact, not forgiveness, nor letting go, nor releasing. The truth that Sarah was not yet able to face was that her father was not a nice man and that he had in fact hurt her very deeply. He continued to hurt her after the rape episodes ended by being cruel and unsupportive. He did other hurtful things in addition to refusing to help her get a car. But Sarah could not yet face her own pain, could not look at her own wounded child.

Your Inner Wounded Child

In order to forgive and to release and let go of a childhood rape, you first have to go within and heal your inner wounded child. When Sarah was saying to me that she had forgiven her father, I wanted to ask, "And now, can I speak to your wounded child?" I have no doubt that her inner wounded child of 10 does not think the father was a nice man. The wounded inner child of 10 knows without a shadow of a doubt that the father was a very cruel man. At this point in the healing of this wounded child, forgiveness should not even be considered. At this point in Sarah's healing she needs to strengthen her boundaries, to begin to dialogue with her inner wounded child. When she feels safe enough, she needs to have the father drawn and quartered and then she needs to direct the anger where it belongs — at the father rather than at the inner wounded child.

For Sarah to get to the top of the mountain, she first has to admit she is still miles from the top, miles from being able to say she has released the pain of the childhood rape. She needs to turn and face her pain which, in truth, despite her protests to the contrary, has not been released.

Unleash The Rage

Sarah could not even admit she had been raped. The person being held accountable by Sarah for the episodes with her father is her inner wounded child. The horrible truth about Sarah, and about every Sarah in the world, is that the man is not blamed, the child is blamed. We, as survivors, need to first forget about forgiveness and need to forget about being nice. We need to unleash the rage that is hidden within, the rage which is holding our inner child hostage. Until the inner wounded child is freed, until the inner wounded child is loved, forgiveness is not even possible.

A few years ago I was watching a television talk show. The talk show host was interviewing a survivor of childhood sexual abuse who was also the author of a book. She mentioned that she had been healing herself for five years and that she had forgiven her father. I stood up in the livingroom and said, "And now let me speak to your wounded child!" The talk show host then received two calls from women who had been raped and they both said they had forgiven the men who had raped them.

We just cannot allow ourselves to get caught up in the passive role of feeling as if we have to forgive such a brutal act. The most important thing to do is to recognize the inner wounded child and to begin the long difficult climb of healing her. I have been dialoguing with my inner wounded child for at least seven years and total forgiveness of the perpetrators has not yet occurred. I would be abandoning my own inner child to pretend I had forgiven.

Finding My Wounded Child

When I was dealing with the pain of a second herniated disc, I began to use an affirmation I had learned from the Louise Hay tapes. I experimented with several affirmations and finally decided to use "I am willing to release the cause of this pain." I chose it because I felt it would cut through any mental resistance to change. I lay in bed with my color lamp on my back and literally said the affirmation hundreds of times a day. Within a few days, while I was in the shower, an image came before me. I saw my own inner wounded child. She was five and she was wrapped in a cocoon where she could not eat or drink. She was dying. As I looked at her and saw her tangled blond hair and her emaciated body, I was engulfed with sadness. I began to cry in deep sobs.

I said to her, "I had no idea, I'm so sorry. All these years I've blamed you for the rape. All these years I've held you accountable. I've held you so accountable that I wanted you to suffer, I wanted you to be in pain. But I didn't know, I really didn't know." I held myself as I talked to the wounded child and sobbed tears of release.

After seven years of dialoguing with my inner child, I had finally come to the deepest layer of pain, I had finally come to the bottom layer of my pit of pain. As I stood there in the shower with the water cleansing my wounds, I understood more than I had ever understood about how deeply hurt I had been when I had been raped at five. I fell to my knees in the shower with the realization that I was dying inside and that the reason I was having thoughts of suicide was that my inner child was, in fact, dying. Also, I realized that the reason I was having real physical pain from the herniated disc was because I was punishing my wounded child for being raped.

I knew that I had to take her out of that cocoon. As I visualized picking her up I imagined the water from the shower cleansing her and awakening her. I held her tight and told her I would never let her go again. I continued to say sweet nothings to her and to love her again. I told her it was not her fault, that she did nothing to cause both men to hurt her. I told her that both men were cruel and that it was their fault that she was raped. I wanted her to know, without a shadow of a doubt, that she was now free and could come out of the darkness into the light.

Within three days the pain started to recede from my leg and the surgery was cancelled. With my inner child healed I no longer had any need for pain.

My Father's Death

Two weeks after the healing of my inner child I heard the lyrics to *The Living Years* by Mike and The Mechanics. As I listened to the song I knew that I needed to see my father, that I needed to do some healing with him while he was still alive. I managed a short visit with my father over the next few weeks but I still felt uneasy about my father's health.

Within two months my father was in a car accident. My sister called and said he was stable. When I said that I would go see him, she told me she did not think it was necessary since we had just seen him. I immediately went back into the role of our childhood and did what my big sister told me. I was uncomfortable with it but I decided to give it a few days.

Two days later, while driving my car and not thinking about anything in particular, I started to hum a tune. I hummed several bars of it and then slowly became conscious of what I was humming. Something about it made me become more alert. When I realized I was humming an old Bee Gees song from the late '60s which I had not heard in years, I knew that I needed to pay better attention to it.

I tried to see if I could remember the lines. Suddenly chills ran up and down my spine. "Getting a message" were the only words I could remember. I immediately went to the nearest record shop and bought a tape of the song. I was trembling when I put the tape in my tape deck. It is a song about a man who is dying who has one more hour to live. In the song the dying man asks the preacher to get a message to a woman and tell her that he is sorry. As I realized that I had just received a message from my dad who was three thousand miles away, I was awestruck.

I immediately called the airlines and booked a flight for the next day. I then called my sister and explained to her that I was going to see Dad because I felt that I had no other choice. The next ten days I stayed at my father's side in the hospital, wiped his brow, fed him and gave him liquid through a straw. My sister immediately joined me when I explained how sick he actually was.

He was aware of my presence the first few days I was there. He was very confused about why I was at his side. I felt the most important single moment was the morning he went into surgery. He was completely aware that morning. Although he was in pain as he was wheeled to the surgical floor, he was calm when my sister and I reassured him that he needed the surgery to get well. When we arrived at the surgery floor, my sister and I had to leave his side. I looked at Dad and I said, "Dad, I want you to know I love you very much and everything is going be fine."

Dad looked at me with complete love in his face, a look that I had not seen in over 30 years. Then we kissed each other. Dad died several days later. I felt an enormous healing of those wounds that had occurred so long ago.

Pain Of Emotional Withdrawal

When Dad raped me, I lost my dad. I lost the father I had loved so much all of my young life. Much of the pain that I experienced in my life was from the physical brutality of the rape but I am also beginning to realize the experience of the pain of the emotional withdrawal of my father after he raped me. All of my life I have tried to get that love back from other men but it never worked. I just kept repeating the cycle of sex and abandonment, always picking emotionally unavailable men.

When I took care of my dying father, I finally got my father back. In front of me was not the strong crazy man who raped me. In front of me was the fragile shell of a man who had his own stories of pain to tell. I do not know why people are so afraid of death. As death comes closer and closer to a person, a softness occurs, a fragility is exposed.

Even though Dad was unable to talk aloud in those days before he died, he did talk to me through his gentleness and through the song, *"I've Got To Get A Message To You."* Anytime I feel I need to hear an apology from my father for the way he treated me, all I now need to do is play the song by the Bee Gees. Psychologist Carl Jung might have said that Dad communicated through the collective unconscious. It was the first time I had knowingly been spoken to in this way when I was awake. I am used to being spoken to in my dreams and I found this experience to be amazing and very healing.

Layer By Layer

In the *Random House College Dictionary,* "forgiveness" is defined as "ceasing to feel resentment against." In my 11 years of healing myself, I have gone through many layers of ceasing to feel resentment against both of my parents, the visiting minister and my own inner wounded child. To give away the resentment, to release the anger, is forgiveness. Instead of holding the anger, instead of living on hate, you gradually learn to let it go, layer by layer by layer.

If I had not healed my wounded child in the months before Dad died, I would not have healed sufficiently to take care of this man who had hurt me so badly. As I sat in the hospital room I remembered how much my father gave me before he began to treat me with so much cruelty. There were many years when my father was kind and loving. I also realized I would not have the strength I presently have if it had not been for my father. I had thrown all of my father out because of the rape. Regaining my father has nothing to do with my father as a separate person. To the contrary, regaining my father is part of my own healing. Mary-the-adult needs to remember the joys, not because of any need to please my father but simply because that was really the way it was.

With my inner wounded child healed, I was able to look at my father with different eyes. Ironically, my father taught me to love more than my mother did. Many of my skills as a mother today were taught me by my father. Releasing layers of pain allowed me to love my father again. Forgiving myself allowed me to see the good in my childhood.

Confrontation

An essential part of the inner forgiveness process for the survivor is, in some manner, to face the perpetrator with his or her abuse. However, deciding to confront the perpetrator is a difficult and complicated process. The level of healing that the survivor has accomplished and the support she has in her life are only two of the considerations. I feel that laying a groundwork is helpful and can provide a kind of safety net for the survivor in case the perpetrator denies the abuse. Part of this groundwork, of course, is therapy. Another part of this groundwork is reacquainting yourself with your family of origin and speaking openly with your brothers and sisters. Finding out, without assuming, what your childhood was like and if your brothers and sisters were also abused can be a very important part of the growth of the survivor and sometimes can be a very real source of unknown support.

If reuniting with brothers and sisters proves not to be supportive, then it can give you a sense of what you might go through when you confront your perpetrator. If you are devastated by meeting with denial or accusations from your siblings, then more therapy might need to occur before you decide to confront your perpetrator.

Completing the story of your childhood by talking to your family of origin can be a very healing experience and can put more of the puzzle pieces together. Another related part of this completion can be to confront the non-incestuous parent first. You can also meet with denial or accusations here, and many survivors begin to doubt themselves when this happens. If the non-incestuous parent and siblings are willing to come into a few therapy sessions with you, sometimes the denial breaks down and small parts of the truth begin to be told. Even a small part of the truth is a monumental experience because the survivor has been so alone in her secret.

I would like to share with you briefly a situation where it appeared that confrontation with the perpetrator failed, but years later the earlier confrontation seemed to actually lay the groundwork for the survivor to enter therapy and finally look at her wounds.

A young girl, whom I will call Beatrice, was being raped almost daily and being sexually abused by her stepfather. Many other brothers and sisters were also encountering the same abuse. An older sister blew the whistle on the abuse and the stepfather was brought to trial. When the case came to trial, Beatrice was the only child who had the courage to continue telling the truth about the abuse. All the other children said they had been lying. Beatrice stood alone in court that day and without backing down faced the defending attorney. The stepfather was acquitted but the real father came and brought Beatrice to live with him. Even though Beatrice was not believed by the court and the perpetrator denied his crime completely, one positive outcome of the confrontation was that the abuse stopped for Beatrice. Today Beatrice is the only adult survivor of more than 14 children who were abused by the stepfather who is in therapy and is actively changing her life. It is my opinion that it was her courageous confrontation in the courtroom combined with the fact that the abuse stopped that freed her to later enter therapy. This is a significant reason why confrontation is so complicated. What may seem on one day like a failure might be laying the groundwork for a more integrated personality at a later time.

Confronting the perpetrator is very personal and each case needs to be decided separately, taking as much information into consideration as possible. In my case I chose not to confront my father. From the age of 36 my father was mentally ill. He was a paranoid schizophrenic and his view of reality was very distorted. He imagined real flesh and blood enemies and he was hospitalized twice in his lifetime. With this distortion of reality I felt certain that my father never remembered raping me and it was my belief that a confrontation would only have led to another hospitalization, which would have led to caretaking problems for my sister and myself. My father had always been able to take care of himself and because of his mental illness we wanted to keep it that way as much as possible.

Confrontation did occur for me, however. It occurred in the individual and group Gestalt therapy. Gestalt therapy is a good arena to experience the pain and the rage with the imagined perpetrator in the room. This confrontation did not occur only once. Untold times I have told my father what he did to me and how wrong and hurtful it was. Rage, sadness, fear, terror, guilt and every other emotion were expressed toward my father in this manner. This style of confrontation brought a gradual healing and I began to feel safe in the world. This confrontation in Gestalt therapy eventually allowed me to forgive my inner child.

Forgive Your Inner Child

Many years ago a person came to us and out of their own darkness and pain they hurt each of us. As children we took on their sins and began to hurt ourselves. Forgiveness — true forgiveness — is now going to our inner wounded child and giving her comfort, giving her love. It is the only forgiveness that matters, the forgiveness we offer our inner wounded child. If, in the process of forgiving the inner wounded child, the incident is released and the perpetrator is forgiven, then that is icing on the cake but never forgive the incident and thereby abandon your inner wounded child. Never fool yourself into thinking that it is more important to forgive the perpetrator than it is to rescue your own inner wounded child.

In healing our wounds of childhood sexual abuse we have embarked on a journey from darkness into light. On this journey we have learned to transform our weaknesses into strengths, our pain into joy and our hate into love. We have done this for only one reason: Somewhere inside the darkness there is a light, somewhere inside us there has always been a light shining, showing us the way. As we walk along our journey, we are walking into ourselves, into our own light. Our journey from darkness into light is our journey home, home to ourselves, home to the inner light that has never gone out. Our journey into light leads us to a new home, to a new place within ourselves that has been there all the time.

Dorothy did make it back to Kansas, and so can we!

PART THREE

The Journey Of
The Heart:
Healing Society

15

The Collective Guilt Of Men

"And the Lord God called to Adam, and said to him, Where are you Adam?
And he said, I heard thy voice in the garden, and when I saw that I was naked, I hid myself.
And the Lord God said to him, Who told you that You were naked? Have you eaten of the tree of which I commanded you that you should not eat?
And Adam said, The woman whom thou gavest to be with me, she gave me of the fruit of the tree, and I did eat."

Genesis 1: 9-12

Over the years, as I began to work on healing myself of the pain from incest, I would from time to time tell people about my history. I noticed a pattern that frequently emerged as I began to tell some men that I was raped as a child. Typically the man would apologize profusely, literally or figuratively grab his genital area, take two steps backwards and never talk to me again. I found myself puzzling over this reaction. It appeared to me that these men were not rapists but they acted guilty. Their apparent feelings of guilt seemed to interfere with their ability to hear more than the first few facts about sexual abuse of children. It appeared to me that if sexual abuse of children was going to end on this planet, then men were going to have to learn how to listen and how to understand the problems and the pain involved for the men, women and children who have been abused.

Collective Guilt of Men

It ultimately occurred to me that the problem might be larger than just a few men feeling guilty that I had been raped. I wondered if I might not be observing something that has actually been held collectively in the unconscious minds of men for centuries — the guilt felt for years by men concerning the manner in which they have treated women and children. The guilt I was observing might be just the tip of the iceberg. I decided to name my observation and to call it the Collective Guilt of Men. By giving it a name and a form, I had hopes of bringing it out into the light to be looked at, dealt with and healed.

I had puzzled for quite some time about the guilt that I had observed in men when I happened to see Joseph Campbell's *The Power of Myth* on public television. He was talking about the myth of Adam and Eve as told in the book of Genesis in the Bible. I realized, as he told the familiar story, that the Collective Guilt of

Men has its seeds in that myth. When God came to Adam and asked him why he ate of the Tree of Knowledge, Adam answered, "Woman gave it to me!" According to this myth, the first man on this earth learned of good and evil from woman! This myth teaches us that the first man on this earth saw his nakedness and the nakedness of woman only after woman gave him the forbidden fruit. He was attracted to the beautiful, soft body of woman because woman tempted him, not because of his own internal yearnings. According to the myth, Adam was sexually attracted to woman because woman gave him the fruit, because woman was desirable. Woman did it!

The Old Testament is the basis of religious thought for the entire Judeo-Christian peoples. The continents of Europe, Australia, North and South America and parts of Africa and Asia all have been populated by people who have been told of Adam and Eve from the time they could talk. Even people who do not go to church or synagogue have the story of Eve tempting Adam heavily embedded in their subconscious mind.

The story of Adam and Eve came out of man's inability to understand the pain of life, and that since we are all born of woman, then woman became the scapegoat. As Joseph Campbell shared, we all came from the womb of a woman. As soon as we are out of the womb, then the pain of a dual world descends upon us. Struggle is part of our world from that moment on. Thus the inner meaning of the myth of Adam and Eve is that pain comes from woman, duality comes from woman, and the sexual feelings inside a man also come from being tempted by woman.

The story of Adam and Eve seen as a myth is accepted by most religions today. Due to advanced knowledge many of us now understand that the Garden of Eden never existed and that Eve never gave Adam a fruit that enlightened him about good and evil. The myth of Adam and Eve was man's attempt to understand his world, and a small world at that. When the myth began to be told from generation to generation, the known world was the land around the Mediterranean Sea. The fact that a myth originally created to define man's small world thousands of years ago still influences our modern world today is a matter of great importance in understanding the present relationships of men and women and of men and children.

Marriage Based On Survival

In the small world of the people inhabiting the world at the time the myth was created, there were no cars, no television, no trip to the moon, no scientific evidence to account for their world. The people then were mainly nomadic with the survival of the clan being supported by the concept of marriage. Without marriage, the small clans would have died out. Marriage, at that time, clearly was not based on love but on survival. Woman was sold to man; they lived together not because they loved each other but because she would bear him children, particularly male children. Male children would seed the earth as they knew it.

Women were property, first of the father and then of the husband. The father of a young girl sold the girl to a man who wanted her. The man and the woman then entered into a legal agreement. Woman would bear his children, work in the fields, make garments and, in general, take care of everything to do with nourishment. This form of marriage was essential to the future of the tribe; without this marriage there would be no children and no tribe.

The Eve Syndrome

Although the present day has little resemblance to this day of tribal customs and marriages, the myth of Adam and Eve has not been replaced. As with many myths, this one strongly affects us by residing in our subconscious minds. According to Bruno Bettelheim, who wrote *Uses of Enchantment,* a fairy tale (or a myth) works subsconsciously and does not require the conscious mind to be aware of its presence. For thousands of years the Judeo-Christian cultures have housed the myth of Adam and Eve in their subconscious minds. For thousands of years the Judeo-Christian cultures have believed the story that Eve did it. Eve caused the pain, Eve caused the temptation and Eve caused man to have knowledge of good and evil.

There are subtle results of the Eve Syndrome that pervade all parts of our culture. In the movie *The Accused,* many people in the bar, as well as in the viewing audience, felt that the woman played by Jodie Foster had asked to be raped because of the way she was dressed and because of the way she danced. This, to me, clearly represents the unconscious part of the Eve Syndrome. The men in the bar felt they were not responsible for their brutal actions because the woman was dressed in a way that showed her sexuality. Woman did it! Eve gave man the apple. Eve tempted man. We are back again to an ancient myth that is still influencing our culture so strongly today.

The woman played by Jodie Foster repeatedly tried to say no but the men did not give her a chance to voice her protests or take any action against the multiple rapes. They brutally raped the beautiful young woman because they were tempted by the woman. Again the influence of the ancient myth was saying that woman is property and that just because woman is sexually attractive, man can do anything he wants with her.

Who we are in the world as moral social beings is directly related to the moral social history of the world. Even though the men who raped the character played by Jodie Foster were not aware of the thousands of years of programming that went into their decision to rape a woman, they, nevertheless, were greatly influenced by the Eve Syndrome and the subsequent societal attitude toward women. In a world where women have been viewed as property for thousands of years, it does not take much of a leap for some men to have little or no regard for her physical boundaries. After all, the earth is our property and we have raped her repeatedly without thought and without remorse.

Sexual abuse of children also has its seeds in the Eve Syndrome. All children, male or female, fall into the category of feminine energy. Little boys are raped before they reach puberty. The pedophiles who rape little boys generally do so when the boys are under the ages of nine or ten, before they are men. Because children are considered to be feminine energy, it follows that men are not responsible for their actions when they rape children; just as Eve did it, the children also bear the guilt of being the tempter. I believe the perpetrator looks at the child as property, as his to do with as he wants.

Our Future

This attitude toward women and children is devastating to the future of our society. Statistically, one out of four women and one out of six men are sexually abused as children. That means one fourth of all women in the United States are struggling against a deep sense of self-hatred and abandonment and one sixth of all men carry similar pain. To take it further, one fourth of all the children raised in America are being mothered by women with little self-worth. Likewise one sixth of all children are being raised by fathers with little self-worth.

Prior to the 1980s it was commonly held that sexually abusing children did not happen very often. Much has been written in the '80s to dispel this myth. Being sexually abused as a child is the most cruel act a child can endure, other than murder and, the truth is, in a sense it *is* murder.

Women Blaming Women

Women also have bought into the Eve Syndrome, the view that women did it, the view that Eve tempted Adam. At one time in their oppression all oppressed peoples agree with their oppressors. That is one of the principal reasons it is so easy for large groups of people to be kept in submission. For some women, the result of the Eve Syndrome is subtle. However, others overtly believe it, just as men do.

Have you ever noticed the reactions of some women when they learn a man has been having an affair? They frequently blame only the woman but not the man who also had the affair. Remember, Eve did it! The man is not held responsible for his sexual feelings, the woman is blamed for tempting the man. Women also have the myth held in their unconscious minds and also participate in keeping it in place.

When women turn against other women they frequently call them the worst possible thing — bitch! Bitch is becoming more commonly used to describe women in movies. It is used more by other women than by men and it is usually used in anger. Women have been so deeply hurt by the Eve Syndrome that when women want to hurt each other they instinctively attack the area where women are the weakest, where they have the least self-worth. A bitch is a female dog who indiscriminately mates with any male dog. The term bitch is now being used as a slang term and according to the *Random House College Dictionary,* it means a "Slang. malicious, unpleasant, selfish woman. a lewd woman."

The word bitch is being used to describe a picture of a woman that would not exist without oppression. A bitch is the direct result of women having been oppressed for these many centuries and is also the direct result of the Eve Syndrome. Women are being seen as angry, critical and immoral. Being a bitch is how we have been hurt. Being a bitch is not something of which to be proud. However, if you call women something other than human, it is easier to treat them other than human.

Eve Did Not Do It

It is time to replace this myth in our subconscious minds. It is time to stop blaming woman for birthing the world. Eve did not do it. Does anyone seriously doubt that there was a man there somewhere? The truth about human beings is that we each are capable of taking total responsibility for our own actions. It is important to stop blaming another person for what we do, think and feel.

Joseph Campbell has also shared his belief that blaming another person for our sins, our actions, is another important part of the myth of Adam and Eve. Adam blamed Eve and Eve blamed the snake! Very few people are willing to take responsibility for their own lives. Apartheid and racism, Hitler's methodical killing of a beautiful race of people and the continuing rape of our beautiful children can find its beginnings in this world-wide myth. The whites in South Africa can blame their problems on the incredibly intelligent and creative black people. The white racists in the world can blame their ills on the blacks and the Jews. And the men and women who still silently rape our children can temporarily feel better as they are taking the life force of a precious child.

The truth is that there is only one way out for the whites of South Africa, there is only one way out for the white racists of the United States and there is only one way out for the men and women who are sexually abusing our children. They all must own up to what they are doing, begin the long journey of self-love and then teach other people how it is done.

It is time for both men and women to take a long hard look at themselves and their attitudes toward women and children and to take responsibility for change within themselves. Women and children are not property, women and children are not disposable commodities. We are all losing by continuing not to take responsibility for our own lives.

Eve did not do it!

16

Healing The Male/ Female Balance On This Earth

Tsegihi.
House made of dawn,
House made of evening light,
House made of dark cloud,
House made of male rain,
House made of dark mist,
House made of female rain,
House made of pollen,
House made of grasshoppers,
Dark cloud is at the door.
The trail out of it is dark cloud.
The zigzag lightning stands high upon it.
Male deity!
Your offering I make.
I have prepared a smoke for you.
Restore my feet for me,
Restore my legs for me,
Restore my body for me,
Restore my mind for me,
Restore my voice for me,
This very day take out your spell for me.

Your spell remove for me.
You have taken it away for me;
Far off it has gone.
Happily I recover.
Happily my interior becomes cool.
Happily I go forth.
My interior feeling cool, may I walk.
No longer sore, may I walk.
Impervious to pain, may I walk.
With lively feelings, may I walk.
As it used to be long ago, may I walk.
Happily may I walk.
Happily, with abundant dark clouds, may I walk.
Happily, with abundant showers, may I walk.
Happily, with abundant plants, may I walk.
Happily, on a trail of pollen, may I walk.
Happily, may I walk.
Being as it used to be long ago, may I walk.
May it be beautiful before me,
May it be beautiful behind me,
May it be beautiful below me,
May it be beautiful above me.
May it be beautiful all around me.
In beauty it is finished.

                                        Navajo Prayer

   The Native Americans understood about the sacred genital area of
both men and women. They created ceremonies to pay homage to
that energy of the body. Creation in general was revered and not
taken for granted. Thanks and gratitude have always been in the
hearts of the Native American for the rain, the soil, the sun, the
seeds, the moon, the seasons and the Great Spirit. Just as the genital
area provides the energy, the fuel, for men and women, so also is
that energy area connected to the energy of all of life. The Native
Americans did not see themselves as separate from the energy of the
Great Spirit or of the sun or of any living thing.

The first people inhabiting this land *knew* they were connected by invisible strings to everything around them. It was impossible for them to look at rivers and plains and the "four-legged" as expendable commodities because they *knew* that made *them* expendable, too. If the rivers dried up or became undrinkable or if the soil on the plains was bleached of nutrients or if the four-leggeds were all killed, then they themselves would die. They would die because the invisible strings that connected their energy center to the energy of the rivers, plains and animals would be destroyed, and they *knew* this. They were aware that the energy of the genital area fueled the energy of their minds and of their hearts. The Native Americans were in balance with their own energy centers which, in turn, were in balance with the energies of the Great Spirit.

A Sacred Place

The genital area for both men and women is a very sacred area. It is an area of creativity. For women, it is the womb of life where a seed is sown and nurtured and, in time, a new human being is born on this earth. However, just as important, the germination of the woman's seed comes from the man. It comes from a very sacred part of the man's body — his genitals. This sacred attitude toward the energy of the genitals, unfortunately, has rarely been part of civilized man's life.

Civilized men have over the centuries been known and revered for their sexual prowess, their physical strength and their thinking abilities, not for their creative sexual energy, their gentleness or their hearts. If men were to change how they use the energy of their genital area and, instead of using it only for sexuality, also learn to use it for the creative energy in their life, a new level of creativity would begin to occur within men. If men would explore the power of the energy of the heart and add this heart energy to their other areas of power, a new relationship would be born between men and women, between men and children and between men and the earth.

The Energy Of The Heart

The energy of thinking is at the top of the body and the energy of sexuality is at the bottom of the trunk. That is a long distance to span if man is struggling with his genital area saying "Sex, sex, sex" and his mind saying "No, no, no." There is truly an easy solution to this conflict. In between the head and the genital area is the heart. In the area of the physical heart there is also the energy center of the emotional heart. This energy is very powerful in the human being. It needs to be cultivated.

An immediate task of the men on this earth is to develop the new energy of the emotional heart and to connect it with the energy of their head and of their genital area. The power, the energy, the fuel is what makes the genital area so vital. The fuel to ignite any idea that the brain can imagine, added to the energy of the emotional heart, gives man balance.

Balance between creation and ideas, balance between female and male and balance between sexuality and love. Within every man is female energy and within every woman is male energy. Since the beginning of time on this earth as we know it, the male/female energy has been out of balance. The result of this imbalance for men has been power without responsibility, sexuality without love and image without self-worth. Unfortunately, this is how men have arrived at the '90s unprepared for intimacy and worshiping sexuality. The result of this imbalance for women has been birth without choice, marriage without love and sex without pleasure. Women have arrived at the '90s without choice and without equality.

Destruction Of The Life Force

Not only do civilized men and women not recognize the sacredness of the life-giving genital areas, they also appear to be unknowingly devaluing them and thereby diminishing their own creative power. One of the worst things you can say to someone today is "fuck you." Almost everyone says it today. When you are truly mad at someone, you give them the finger or even better, the entire arm. The fascinating part about this act of saying, "Fuck you" is that the basis of saying it comes from the ancient knowledge hidden in our subconscious that the genital area is our source of creative energy. By saying, "Fuck you" to the person we are angry with at the moment, we all believe that it, in fact, takes their power away. It takes their power away at the deepest level possible, at the level where our strings are attached to all of life. This is now even being depicted in the movies.

For instance, in a number of movie scenes, a person is found pointing a gun at a man's head and demanding information. The man in peril of having his head shot off firmly will not talk. If the one with the gun, however, points it at the man's genitals, the man in peril suddenly cannot talk fast enough. Most of us tend to believe that the fast talking is a direct result of men worshiping their genitals.

I believe it is on a much deeper level than fear of castration. Each of us *knows* where our creative energy comes from, but that knowledge is not in our conscious mind. When someone points a gun at a man's genitals, he realizes that his very life force is at stake.

Likewise, when a child or a woman is raped, it is the life force of that child or woman that is damaged. The act of rape results in men taking the creative energy from children and women, taking the source of our power from us. Men who rape are men who have diminished self-worth and whose own creative source of power is not available to them. They feel they are in a power struggle with the opposite sex for their very survival. They feel that they have to rape, they have to destroy the creative energy source of the female and take it for themselves.

The Child's Creative Life Force

The men who rape children have issues that are different from the men who rape women. The sexual attraction to children who are not overtly sexual comes from a deep hatred from within the man, a hatred so strong that the man feels he must destroy the beautiful life force every child displays. These men want to drink in the beautiful life force of the children. These men understand on a deep level where the life force comes from but they do not realize they can get it from within themselves. They are not attracted to the sexuality, which is not there yet. They are, however, attracted to the creative life force of the child.

If men who rape children would only begin to heal themselves by slowly and courageously taking steps toward self-love, then their attraction to the life force of the child would end and they could live in harmony with the beautiful children of our planet.

Balance

Throughout history many men have taken wives to keep the feminine energy in their lives, to have nurturance, to have balance. Also many women have taken husbands to balance their feminine side, to give form to their softness, realization to their dreams. The Women's Liberation Movement was about equality but it was also about balance. Women were saying that the world was out of balance and that it was time to get it back into balance.

If men gradually will begin to claim their feminine side, to nurture themselves, to develop their vision, to develop their hearts, they will then find balance within themselves. If women will begin to learn to activate their dreams, to take action in the world, to bring their visions into reality, they will then also find balance within themselves. This is a new balance, this a new way of relating for human beings. Instead of balancing the male/female energy by a marriage that limits the expression of both the man and the woman, that confines the man into providing/activating energy and confines the woman into nurturing energy, a new balance is now available to us. An internal balance of male and female energies, a happiness that has not been known on this earth could be about to be born.

Men and women will still be attracted to each other but instead of men depending on the woman for the tending of his heart and his nurturance, he will tend his own heart and provide himself with his own nurturance. The man can now learn an entirely new level of love, the ecstasy of which has not been known on this planet. With his male energy balanced with his own female energy, he will no longer be hungry for nurturance, he will no longer be excessively hungry for the creative life force of another. His emotional heart will open and a new love will begin to emerge, not based on hunger but based on contentment. With this new love it will then be impossible to abuse our children, our women or our earth. With this new love, men will learn to create in an entirely new way, in balance with Mother Earth.

Also, with this new internal balance, women will stop looking to men for their form, for the energy to activate their dreams. Women will connect with their innate ability to dream, to have vision and then, by using their own newly found male energy, will take their visions into the world. Women will find they can create more than just babies from their womb of visions. If women stay in touch with their feminine energy, they will create a world without pollution, without crime and without abuse and Mother Earth will rotate contentedly on her axis.

17

The Equality of Women

Dream

I was standing in the middle of an ancient valley. Surrounding the valley were tall jagged mountain peaks. I could tell that the mountains were billions of years old because of the type of rock visible in the mountains. Many Indian women were in the valley. Some were working in the fields, some were playing drums and some were dancing. As I watched, an old Indian woman appeared among the women and suddenly the women formed a circle and began to dance together. I joined with them. Later the old Indian woman came to me and gave me a piece of gold about the size of my hand. On it was the design of a woman's face. She told me to keep the treasure.

Historically, people who have been oppressed must reach a point in their growth where they know they are worthwhile as human beings and where they know that they should no longer be dominated by their oppressors, before they will fight for their freedom. No oppressor in the history of man has suddenly said, "We really shouldn't be oppressing these people any longer, let's let them go!" The turning of the tide generally occurs from within the hearts of the group that has been dominated when that group collectively calls upon its courage to win its freedom.

I was quite distressed when we as a nation could not pass the Equal Rights Amendment for women. African Americans had passed their amendment years before the defeat of the ERA. They knew within their hearts they were equal to anyone. What, then, prevents women from knowing that? What is different in the way we have been oppressed?

Women And Oppression

African Americans have been oppressed for about four hundred years, while women have been oppressed for *thousands* of years. Prior to being taken into bondage, the African American people were a proud and free people who had effective tribal governments and religions that connected them to the true life force. Women do not have that wonderful rich history from which to draw. Women do not have a memory in their subconscious minds of being a free and proud group of people.

Another difference in the oppression of women is that many women choose to be in a love relationship with the very people who are oppressing them. Through marriage, women are also in a legal contract with the sex who has dominated them for centuries.

Women are tied economically and emotionally to the group of people who have prevented them from holding equal jobs for equal pay and who have viewed them as property.

Anger assisted the Civil Rights Movement. Because those belonging to the African American community were not emotionally attached to their oppressors, it was easier for them to reach their anger and use it effectively in the world. They were economically attached to the white community but, fortunately for their freedom, they were not in a love relationship with the white community. It is very difficult to reach anger when it is confused with love.

A Time Of Transition

At this point in our history men and women are in a stage of transition. Transition from many centuries of viewing one another as less than each of us actually is. Transition from many centuries of viewing our relationship as economic, and transition from many centuries of viewing our relationship as being based on fear. Transition is a difficult time. It is a time when fear and anger are prevalent because the past, although not beneficial for either party, was a known and familiar territory and the future is unknown and very uncertain.

Moontime

To understand how the devaluation of women has affected the very essence of who we are, it is important to look at that part of us which makes us a woman — our womb. When I visited the Seneca Nation during the Harmonic Convergence, Twylah Nitsch, an elder and wise woman, taught me many things that I have never forgotten. One of her teachings concerned the cycle of women — our menstrual cycle. Twylah taught me that the Native American people on this continent used the word *moontime* to signify when women were having their menstrual cycles. Just as the moon has her phases, so also do women have theirs. During this period of time, the sisters and the woman's husband would take over the work load for the woman and she would usually go into the woods or other secluded place to have her quiet time. The quiet time and seclusion were made available to her because these people were aware of the increased perception of the woman during this phase of her moon cycle.

During the time the blood was flowing from the woman's uterus there was a heightened awareness in the woman. If she went into meditation, she would often see visions and have deep understandings. She was respected by her people for her increased capacity for intuition and, thus, not only was she honored but, also, her creative energy-giving genital area was honored.

Now let us compare this to the current attitude of the American woman toward her menstrual cycle. For generations the American woman has called it "the curse," "being on the rag" or "Oh, my god, it's my period again" and then they have run to the medicine cabinet and taken little pills to help them forget they are "on the rag again."

Instead of honoring this phase of the woman's life, it is being denied. It is being so denied and devalued that the energy center that surrounds the area has changed. When the genital area of the woman is honored, she also honors the creative energy of that area — the life force. When the genital area is not honored, the creative energy of that area — the life force — is altered. Disease can then begin in that area. Cancer of the uterus, infertility, cysts, tumors, premature births, difficult births, death of the fetus . . . the list goes on forever. It is a high price to pay for our attitude toward ourselves as women.

A major change needs to occur in women's attitudes toward their *moontime,* their menstrual cycle. By denying this time, we are denying our time of visions, our intuitive time.

First, we are women. First, we are creators. First, we are people of vision.

It is time to go back to being women but not women who accept oppression. It is time to find a new womanhood, a womanhood based on who we truly are — creators of life, carriers of the womb of vision.

Honoring Our Cycles

The Native American women understood that a woman has phases, cycles like the moon. The moon is female and has cycles. The sun is male and does not have cycles. Both women and men find it difficult to change. Perhaps with women and men getting better in touch with their feminine sides, change will come more easily to all of us.

The Native American woman used moss from the earth to absorb the blood during her moon cycle. When it was full, she would put it back in the earth and take another piece of the soft clean moss, giving thanks to Mother Earth.

Gratitude was part of the foundation of the Native American way of life. They gave thanks for the sun and the moon and for the contributions to their life from the earth. In this way they never forgot their connections to everything on this planet earth.

In finding our new womanhood we need to express gratitude to our moontime, to our phases, to our cycles. Without the influence of the moon on our lives, we would not find it easy to change, to grow. Our moontime has many lessons that we have been unable to see because we have rejected the blood and the discomfort. Instead of rejecting the cycle of menstruation, give it honor and gratitude. Accept its cycles as symbolic of our ability to change and to grow. Honor the genital area and begin to use the energy of that area for more than sexuality. Begin to use the energy of that area for creativity in your lives. Just watch how fast things begin to change for the better in your lives when you begin to honor your cycle of change. If the cycle of change is honored, then positive creative change can easily occur in your life.

Responsibility

It is time to take stock of our gains and losses for both women and men and to balance our books. We need to live in the '90s with a better understanding of what it means to be a woman and what it means to be a man. Being equal means that women have the same rights to economic independence, the same rights not to be physically and sexually abused and the same rights as to choice of how we live our lives.

The time is long overdue for us to begin releasing our fear and anger and to stop projecting our frailties onto the people who are different. It is time for each person to take responsibility for his or her own existence and to make the necessary changes for global human rights. If we do not start thinking globally and protecting our human rights, we are at risk. We are at greater risk than at any other time in the history of man because if mankind does not develop its emotional heart, the misuse of power will continue. Our air will not be breathable, our water will not be drinkable, our food will not nourish us and our children will continue to be abused.

The female is the nourisher, the renewer of life. It is our very essence. We hold the womb within us. Women have the task to awaken within all of us our femaleness, our creativity, and to nourish and heal ourselves, our children and, then, Mother Earth.

The male is the provider, without whom life would not continue. The male provides the sperm, the activator for our silent seeds of life. Men now have the task to activate their emotional hearts for a new experience in relating to women and children, to the Mother Earth and to the Great Mystery. Without the emotional heart being activated, the male power will continue without boundaries and without responsibilities. Without the emotional heart, activated men will continue to look to women for the energy of their heart and to children for their creative life force.

". . . Certain Inalienable Rights"

As long as the rights of any group of people on this earth are denied, then humanity as a whole is diminished.

As long as the rights of women are denied, then men are diminished.

As long as the rights of Jews, African Americans and Native Americans are denied, then the United States is diminished.

As long as the rights of children are denied, all of mankind is diminished.

Our nation was built on the truth that all peoples are created equal. As long as any one group of people is treated unequally, then the nation as a whole is undermining its own solid foundation of truth.

Bibliography

The Accused. Dir. Jonathan Kaplan. Paramount Pictures. 1988.

Bee Gees. "I've Got To Get A Message To You." Written by Gibb, Gibb & Gibb. Polygram Records, Inc., 1976.

Beethoven, Ludwig Von. Symphony No. 9 in D Minor, op. 125.

Bettelheim, Bruno. **The Uses of Enchantment.** New York: Vantage, 1977.

Campbell, Joseph. "The Power of Myth with Bill Moyers." 1988. Apostrophe S Productions, in association with Public Affairs Television, Inc. and Alvin H. Perlmutter, Inc. Series Producer: Joan Konner and Alvin H. Perlmutter. Exec. Ed. Bill Moyer, #2, 4.

Close Encounters of the Third Kind. Dir. Steven Spielberg. 1977.

Cocker, Joe. "You Are So Beautiful." Written by B. Preston and B. Fisher. A&M Records, Inc., 1972.

Davis, Adelle. **Let's Get Well.** New York: Harcourt, Brace & World, 1965.

Garfield, Leah Maggie. **Sound Medicine.** Berkeley: Celestial Arts, 1987.

Hay, Louise. *You Can Heal Your Life.* Santa Monica: Hay House, 1985.

"Healing Wounded Child Workshop." Pat Rodegast. Creative Options, Springhouse, Pennsylvania, Oct. 1987.

Holy Bible. Philadelphia: A. J. Holman, 1957.

Jung, Carl. **Man and His Symbols.** New York: Laurel, 1964.

Merriam Webster Dictionary. New York: Simon & Schuster.

Mike and the Mechanics. "The Living Years." Written by Mike Rutherford and B. A. Robertson. Atlantic Recording Corp., 1988.

Miller, Melinda and Jane Rachfalski. "Rainbow Dancer" (in manu-
script), Light Works & Co., #2 Providence Forge, Royersford,
Pennsylvania, 1968.

Momaday, N. Scott. **House Made of Dawn.** New York: Harper & Row,
1966.

Morrison, Van. "Listen to the Lion." Written by Van Morrison. Warner
Bros. Records, 1972.

Nitsch, Twylah. Summer 1987 Intensive. Wolf Clan Teaching Lodge,
Cattaraugus Indian Reservation, 12199 Brant Reservation Road,
Brant, N.Y. 14027-0136.

"Orpheus." Dir. Jean Cocteau. With Jean Marais. 1949, France.

Random House College Dictionary. New York: Random House, 1984.

Robbins, Marty. "The Hanging Tree." Written by M. David and Jerry
Livingston. Warner Brothers Picture: "The Hanging Tree," 1958.

Sams, Jamie and David Carson. **Medicine Cards.** Sante Fe: Bear and
Company, 1988.

Sechrist, Elsie. **Dreams: Your Magic Mirror.** New York: Warner, 1968.

Simon, Paul. "Graceland." Warner Bros. Records, 1986.

Sutphen, Dick. "Peaceful Sleep Programming." Valley of the Sun
Audio/Visual, Box 3004, Agoura Hills, California 91301.

Williamson, Chris. "Lullaby." Written by Chris Williamson. Olivia
Records: The Dream Machine, 1978.

Wizard of Oz. Dir. Victor Fleming, 1939.

Wonder, Stevie. "A Place In the Sun." Written by R. Miller and B.
Wells. Motown, 1966.

Appendix

Light Works & Co.: Books, Tapes and Color Lamp, #2 Providence
Forge, Royersford, Pa. 19468

Twylah Nitsch: Wolf Clan Teaching Lodge, Cattaraugus Indian Reservation, 12199 Brant Reservation Road, Brant, N.Y. 14027-0136.

ENHANCE YOUR RECOVERY

With Changes Magazine — America's Leading Recovery Publication

Discover the magazine that gives you the vital self-healing tools you need to understand your inner self and recover from a traumatic past.

Each copy of **Changes** brings essential information on personal recovery concerns like self-esteem, intimacy, relationships and self-parenting. Plus you'll receive news on support groups, new recovery techniques, and insights from featured personalities like Oprah Winfrey, John Bradshaw and Leo Buscaglia.

Move ahead in your recovery and try Changes now with our unconditional money-back guarantee. Just return the coupon below or call toll-free 1-800-851-9100.

Yes, please begin my subscription to **Changes** Magazine. If I'm unsatisfied I can cancel my subscription within 30 days after I receive my first issue and promptly receive a full refund. After 30 days, I'm guaranteed a full refund on all unmailed issues.

Name _____
(please print)

Address _____ Apt. _____

City _____ State _____ Zip_____

Payment: ___ 1 Year $18.00 (6 Issues)   ___ 2 Years $34.00 (12 Issues)
___ Mastercard ___ Visa ___ Check (Payable to **The U.S. Journal**)

Acct. No. _____

Exp. Date _____ Signature _____

Response Code HDCHG2

CALL TOLL-FREE 1-800-851-9100 TO CHARGE BY PHONE

SEND TO: The U.S. Journal Inc./Subscriptions
3201 SW 15th St.
Deerfield Beach, FL 33442-8190